P9-CSA-754

Keeping the Faith
Making a Difference

Fr. Miscamble's commitment to inspire young minds and souls with the wisdom of the Catholic tradition reaches far outside the classroom. Here, he reads the "signs of the times" in light of the gospel call to *be light* for the world, offering a direct challenge to young Catholics to view the world through the lens of faith—not vice versa.

Kristin Sadie
Pastoral Associate and Director of
Young Adult Ministry
Holy Name Cathedral, Chicago

Reading *Keeping the Faith, Making a Difference* is akin to the joyful experience of knowing Fr. Bill Miscamble as a priest, teacher, and friend. In his humorous and gently persistent way, he challenges his readers to become better citizens, by loving their neighbors as Christ did, with "heroic self giving."

Allison Fuss
Assistant Professor
United States Naval Academy

Fr. Bill opens his heart in these priceless bits of encouragement and advice. His enormous love for his faith, his students, his teaching, the church, and the priesthood is abundantly clear on each page. Fr. Bill's courage to share his beliefs so openly has inspired me to examine my own life and has challenged me to focus my efforts on how I can not only keep my faith, but authentically live it as well.

Jonathan Lang
Teacher with the Alliance
for Catholic Education

Twenty-something college graduates can find the transition from a nurturing and supportive undergraduate community into a more complex and uncertain post-college world at times confusing and even a bit frightening. *Keeping the Faith, Making a Difference* is a useful guide for this journey. It helps one to reflect on the importance of faith and true ideals, and calls one to build on those ideals as a Catholic adult.

Laura G. Holland
University of Notre Dame Graduate,
Class of 1998

Keeping the Faith
Making a Difference

WILSON D. MISCAMBLE, C.S.C.

ave maria press Notre Dame, Indiana

© 2000 by Ave Maria Press, Inc.

All rights reserved. No part of this book may be used or reproduced in any manner whatsoever, except in the case of reprints in the context of reviews, without written permission from Ave Maria Press, Inc., P.O. Box 428, Notre Dame, IN 46556.

International Standard Book Number: 0-87793-933-0

Cover and text design by Katherine Robinson Coleman

Printed and bound in the United States of America.

Library of Congress Cataloging-in-Publication Data

Miscamble, Wilson D,
     Keeping the faith, making a difference/Wilson D. Miscamble.
     p.   cm.
     Includes bibliographical references.
     ISBN 0-87793-933-0 (pbk.)
     1. Christian life—Catholic authors. 2. Young adults—Religious
life. I. Title
     BX2355 .M55 2000
     248.8'34—dc21   99-048595
                                    CIP

To my students

with gratitude

Contents

Acknowledgments

At the outset I must thank all the young men and women with whom I have had the opportunity to minister as a priest-teacher over the past decade and a half. I must mention especially those who have been my students as well as the members of the communities in Badin, Zahm, O'Neill, and Breen-Phillips Halls where I have presided and preached regularly. I am grateful for their friendship to me and for their Christian witness and commitment which helped inspire this book. The dedication is but a token of my gratitude.

In writing the book I have acquired debts to a number of people which I wish to acknowledge, although, of course, the responsibility for its contents remains with me. Jonathan Lang served as my "chief-of-staff" during 1998-1999. He read the manuscript with great care and commented on it in helpful ways as did three wonderful young women and good friends—Laura Holland, Allison Fuss, and Liz Trantowski. They each gave me needed assurance that this book was "worth reading." I also appreciated the comments on sections of the manuscript offered by Theresa Hennessey and by the participants in Fr. Pat Neary's Hispanic student retreat group.

Good friends and confreres in the Congregation of Holy Cross also lent me their encouragement and assistance. Fr. Charles Gordon read the entire manuscript thoroughly for style and content and offered very insightful comments. Frs. Tom Blantz, Jim King, and Pat Neary also commented on the text. My provincial, Fr. Bill Dorwart, read the manuscript and encouraged its publication. I thank him for that and for assigning me to spend my "sabbatical year" at Moreau Seminary at Notre Dame where I wrote the book.

At Ave Maria Press, Frank Cunningham, Bob Hamma, and, especially, Julie Hahnenberg assisted in the preparation and production of this book. It has been a pleasure to work with them. I also thank Kari Kloos for her careful proofreading of the manuscript. Margaret Jasiewicz of the Decio Faculty Services Office at Notre Dame went out of her way to assist me in preparing the manuscript to submit to the Press and I am very grateful to her.

In a more general way I want to thank Dan and Mary Ann Rogers of South Bend, Indiana, and Mrs. Alice Rogers of Edina, Minnesota, for their generous support of my work. It is truly appreciated. Last, I want to thank my Mum and Dad, who are both mentioned in this book, and my sister and brother, Jenny and Phillip, for their love and example. Their faith strengthens mine.

WILSON D. (BILL) MISCAMBLE, C.S.C.
NOTRE DAME, INDIANA

Introduction

This is a simple book about some significant matters. It is a treatment of some basic ideas and practices in Christian belief and life. It is written primarily for Catholic students attending colleges and universities and for recent graduates of such institutions. With this special audience in mind, it initially addresses some familiar aspects of Christian faith and discipleship: God's love for us, the centrality of Jesus Christ, our shared call as disciples, the importance of the eucharist and of informed faith, and the task of resisting temptation. Next it addresses a number of more personal issues which my student friends have raised to me in varying ways at one time or another: facing suffering, true friendship, love and sex, marriage, the challenges of Christian manhood and womanhood today, and the responsibilities of parenting.

My hope is that this series of brief reflections might encourage young Catholic women and men to participate ever more vigorously in the church's mission on earth. To this end the book includes in its third section some short treatments of a number of crucial societal issues and explores how today's young adults might live their Christian vocations in the world. It asks how young Catholics might engage well in the vital work of evangelization. Although related, each reflection might be read as a discrete piece. I hope that they might be read (and reread) as time and circumstances demand.

This little book had its genesis in the occasional requests of students for a copy of a talk or reflection. They are getting a bit more than they asked for. That said, however, they (and other readers) are hardly faced here with a lengthy tome. I trust that these brief reflections will give encouragement, challenge, reassurance, and even inspiration in living the Christian life. These essays grow out of talks, reflections, and homilies given at the University of Notre Dame where I teach history and minister in the residence halls. My greatest association with college students has been on that campus, and, naturally, I hope these essays might be of some interest to students there—past, present, and future. But I trust they also might be of benefit to young women and men in other Catholic schools and in private and public colleges and universities across the United States and even beyond it. Students and recent graduates everywhere face compelling yet common questions about what to believe and whom to trust. They confront similar and critical choices about vocations, relationships, and values.

As will be obvious from the outset, these reflections are not offered in some contrived form to reflect the lingo of either "Generation X" or its emerging successor, dubbed "Generation Y" by some. I have found in my years of ministry on a college campus that young women and men better appreciate plain and direct speech reflecting honest views and authentic sentiment. I pray readers will find exactly this in the pages which follow written by a middle-aged, Australian priest quite unskilled in the art of prevarication. My reflections borrow from or are inspired by many different sources, both directly and indirectly. The scriptures are the most notable inspiration and departure point. Other significant works which guided my thinking are acknowledged in a separate note at the end of the book.

My area of scholarly research centers on postwar American foreign policy, and I have written at some length on that subject. This is a different kind of writing venture for me. In pursuing it I have sensed deeply that I responded to the specific call in the Constitutions of the

Congregation of Holy Cross (my religious order) to be an "educator in the faith." Ultimately, as I know only too well from my own efforts at teaching, the work of education is done best when we learn together. Writing these reflections benefited my faith and deepened my desire to respond to God's unfailing love for me. I hope the same reaction might be shared by those who read these words of introduction and the essays which follow.

Faith &
Discipleship

God's Call & Our Worth

"Be not afraid, follow me."

It seems that self-esteem, or rather the lack of it and the need for it, is always in the news. Our society is pervaded by complaints that young women and men suffer greatly from a lack of self-esteem. Some folks even argue that history texts must be written in such a way as to build the esteem of today's students. Students, it is argued, should have their worth affirmed by what they learn of the past. The matter, however, goes far beyond history texts. The self-help shelves at your local bookstore are filled with books on this subject. These books have titles like *The Confidence Factor: How Self-Esteem Can Change Your Life*.

You may have seen literature from the campus counseling center which draws attention to the problem. It is a problem that can be manifested in a variety of ways. The lack of self-esteem, it seems, is more likely to affect women than men, but it is important to note that the problem is not peculiar to women. Both men and women can get caught in a trap of looking outward rather than inward for self-esteem. Both men and women get caught up in the need for rewards, strokes, and accomplishments to confirm their worth. Both women and men get caught up in the social pressures of appearance—valuing themselves largely by how they look.

I'm not going to pretend I have the answer to the problem in all its various dimensions. I'm certainly not going to recommend a "self-help" book to you. Rather, I want to suggest that scripture has something important to say to us about self-esteem and self-worth.

The Gospel of Luke (5:1-11) records a fascinating episode when Jesus tells Simon Peter, who had been fishing all night and caught nothing, to lower his nets again. When he did, such was the catch that the boat was almost pulled under. Thereupon Simon Peter shouted out, "Leave me, Lord. I am a sinful man." He felt himself unworthy because it suddenly struck him that he was in the company of God. Peter is not alone in this kind of reaction. Lots of folk find it difficult to be near God. Perhaps we might be like Simon Peter and feel ourselves unworthy. But it is instructive to look at the response which greeted Simon. He was greeted not with criticism of his unworthiness but rather with a charge from God, with a call. Jesus greeted Simon tenderly and said, "Be not afraid, follow me, and you will catch men and women together with me."

Peter responded to the call—and this same call comes to each of us. Of course we can be pretty skilled in our attempts to deny it. We can use our very "unworthiness" as a shield to hide behind. Surely God is not calling me! But the answer is YES! God knows of our weaknesses, our limitations, and our sins. But God's grace and favor can transform us and allow us to respond to his call. It is this transformation which we seek when we pray at communion time: "Lord, I am not worthy to receive you, but only say the word and I shall be healed."

Our basic worth was established at the moment of our conception when God called us into being—with an assist from our moms and dads. Our essential worth and dignity as persons was immediately established. We didn't have to do anything special or look a particular way. From our conception and birth onward God treasures us as his own. Each of us is a child of God. This status never changes, no matter how old we get. But God calls to each of us and gives us the opportunity to obtain our full worth by living to our highest potential. This is the way to the deepest "self-esteem." God gives us our worth and dignity at the outset and asks us to be fully with him. My friends, however you feel about yourself right now, be not afraid— follow the Lord.

Jesus Lord & the Scriptures

I read an article recently which suggested that religion teachers all over the country give the scriptures, and especially the gospels, to intelligent and sensitive students, but without much response. Few students, it seems, are stirred in any special way by the good news proclaimed by Jesus and recorded in the accounts of Matthew, Mark, Luke, and John. Reading, for example, that one should yield first place to others and take the last place or that one is to love God and one's neighbor with the same care and concern we lavish on ourselves apparently doesn't really connect. All of that stuff happened long, long ago and, it seems, in a galaxy far, far away. Jesus, the main actor in the gospel drama, becomes a somewhat distant figure. He might be considered a decent fellow but a bit of a do-gooder who can be safely dismissed.

It is when we begin to drift toward this nonchalant attitude to the scriptures that we need to zero in anew on the essence of our faith convictions. Then is the time when we might locate ourselves beside that good and feisty woman, Martha, and confess to Jesus: "I believe that you are the Messiah, the Son of God" (Jn 11:27). We need to profess that JESUS IS LORD! This Jesus is the one whom God raised from the dead. This is the Christian's central belief. It is the source of our salvation.

Jesus is the indispensable figure of history. He had no great armies, nor did he engage in the conquest of nations. He spent his public life simply teaching and healing and reaching out to those who felt abandoned and afraid. The fulfillment of his life on earth came when he freely and obediently chose to suffer and to die. He died largely despised—an outcast and accursed—clearly a dispensable figure to the civil and religious authorities of his time. Yet, he died so that we might live. His death opened the way for life. He proved to be, as he had promised Martha, "the resurrection and the life" who opens the possibility of life in its fullness to each of us.

When we profess this faith in Jesus as Lord and Savior not only with our lips but also in our hearts, we respond to the gospel and resist the temptation to stand alone and independent of our God. This temptation, it seems, is a primal one. Adam and Eve first succumbed to it in the garden. And the scriptures (Luke 4:1-13) vividly remind us that no one escapes this primal temptation—not even Jesus himself. The Spirit led Jesus into the desert for forty days. This experience, with its culminating series of temptations, proved to be the crossroads of his life. Here lay a crisis for him. He had to decide between two ways open before him. The devil offered Jesus smooth travel on the much-favored path of self-reliance and "success." Power and fame could be his.

Jesus chose instead to follow a less traveled and more rocky pathway. This was a way that clashed with conventional wisdom of who and what a Messiah should be. And it is well to remember that all through his life and even into his final hours, Jesus would continue to hear the tempter's insistent words. This is important for us to appreciate because, like Jesus, we, most likely, are tempted quite frequently to stand outside of God's world. This temptation can be subtle and rather satisfying. We can be tempted by what is not obviously evil, and therein lies our struggle. We unthinkingly give ourselves over to today's "consumerist addiction" and to the "celebrity cult" and quickly find our lives ruled by a weird combination of seductive advertising and imitation of the "famous." Our focus is on "keeping up" with everyone else—the mall, the car, the clothes, the attitudes.

Who among us has not at some point in our lives constructed a domain which we control, on which we focus and from which God is excluded? We build our reputations, secure our status or possessions, try to gain some power or fame. We are not doing anything especially wrong. We are driven more by the need to soothe our inner turmoil and insecurities than by explicitly bad motives. But these domains become, in a way, our secret gods. They are what and where we really worship.

We know these temptations exist and will continue in various forms. That is why we must engage the scriptures constantly and let them challenge and guide us. They must be our required reading for life. They can bring us to a crossroads in our lives and help us expose the secret gods within. They can help turn us toward the path trod by Jesus—the path of ever deepening trust in God. They will draw us to profess on our lips and in our hearts that JESUS IS LORD.

"Whoever
does not carry
the cross and
follow me
cannot be
my disciple."

Discipleship for Others

The gospels at times force us to confront squarely the costs of discipleship of the Lord Jesus. For example, what are we to make of these ringing challenges from the Gospel of Luke (14:25-33):

▼ "Whoever does not carry the cross and follow me cannot be my disciple."

▼ "Whoever does not hate father and mother, spouse and children, brothers and sisters, yes, and even life itself, cannot be my disciple."

▼ "None of you can become my disciple if you do not give up all your possessions."

Can these demanding strictures possibly apply to us? It all seems a bit harsh and overdone, don't you think? Surely it asks more of us than we are prepared to give or are even capable of giving.

And yet our willingness to hear the gospel suggests that we are prepared at least to consider these powerful demands of being a Christian disciple. I want to propose to you that reflecting upon and acting upon this call to discipleship should be central to your education. You are talented, and are receiving good training in engineering or business or pre-med or psychology or whatever. But if you journey through your studies without seeing this time as a crucial period in your life to respond to the call to discipleship, your time will have been tragically wasted. And this will be the case no matter whether you finish with a four-point average, with fellowships to great graduate programs, or with lucrative offers from major employers. You will have missed the opportunity to tap into the richest and most crucial wisdom, namely the wisdom of Jesus Christ.

But this is not something we can do in a half-hearted or wimpish way. If we are going to be disciples, we have to lay firm foundations and commit our lives over the long haul. Our response to the gospel must have the first place and be the compass that guides our lives—more important than possessions; more important even than family and loved ones; even more important than life itself. Indeed we must give of our lives to follow Jesus.

Now all this is pretty abstract, I know. You've been listening to talks and homilies for years and priests rambling on about discipleship and putting God at the center of our lives and so forth—yada, yada, yada! Perhaps you ask: How in practical terms is this to be done? How can I tap into that true wisdom that saves?

There are of course many ways, like prayer and service. Prayer—especially the eucharist—joins you with the Christian community in praise and worship of God. Service allows you to put your gifts and talents at the disposal of others in need. We should structure prayer and service into our days and weeks and make them part of our lives. But here I want to suggest that a key way in which you can respond more deeply to the call to discipleship lies in how you relate to other people.

We happen to live in a period when men and women with our opportunities and possibilities have an overwhelming sense of entitlement. We expect a lot, not so much of ourselves but for ourselves. This is in many ways still the era of "if it feels good, do it." Our associations with others can be determined essentially by how much they contribute to our pleasure and supposed well-being. Now this sort of attitude is easy to recognize in certain types of folks. For example, the young woman obsessed with her appearance, her standing and place among others, who chooses her friends on the basis of what they can do for her, who talks of them readily behind their backs and distances herself from them if it seems advantageous. Or there's the incorrigible young man, the sort of narcissist type impressed with his own accomplishments and for whom other people, especially women, are mere instruments and objects. There are such types around, I'm afraid to say.

For such folk, other people are merely to be used in a vain quest to satisfy some insatiable emptiness within themselves. But, in sharp contrast, faithful and authentic Christian women and men treat each other and all those they meet as true brothers and sisters in the Lord. They have no hint of superiority in how they think of others. They don't approach anyone with base motives but relate to one another with integrity and honesty and charity. They do the little things that make discipleship live.

For those of us at college, discipleship means that we must genuinely welcome newcomers and comfort them during the episodes of loneliness or anxiety that sometimes come. We must make sure no one eats alone or is left out. We must build up and deepen the bonds of community and resist the harmful tendencies to compare and to compete. We must ensure that those who make mistakes are forgiven. We must support and encourage each other in living our Christian beliefs and commitments.

With God's help, we disciples can give more than we ever imagined possible if we have the wisdom to discern the gospel challenge and the courage to respond to it.

> "Let us live
> in such a
> way
> That when
> we die
> Our love
> will survive
> And
> continue
> to grow."

Faith Across the Generations

I regularly teach a course called "The Development of Modern America" to first-year students. Now, to allow the students to adjust both to my accent and to the rather odd fact that they are in an American history course being taught by an Australian, I begin with a little "homilette" on the importance of history. I ramble on to the effect that while history might not provide us with explicit answers to our present questions, it can give us a perspective of sorts—even a certain wisdom—in dealing with them. And, for a little rhetorical flourish, I quote an aphorism, derived from Cicero I believe: "Who knows only his own generation remains forever a child."

I then suggest to the class that we will attempt to trace the historical experience of generations other than our own so as to deepen our perspective and to aid our growing-up.

Now analyzing the different "generations" has become a bit of a fad in the United States in recent years. Social scientists and cultural commentators and the ubiquitous poll-takers all try to define the character and characteristics of each generation and to outline the contours of generational conflict. This generational analysis received a boost with the 1992 presidential election. Here the torch was passed to a representative of the baby-boom generation—roughly those born from the mid-1940s to the mid-1960s. The new president replaced the last of the World War II era presidents, a representative of a great group of Americans born in the first two decades of this century who came of age during the Great Depression. The men of that generation went away to fight and came home to marry, to create with their wives a life for their children far better than they themselves had experienced, forging in the process intensely child-focused households and communities. They are, in the main, the senior citizens of today, perhaps your grandparents.

But now the boomers are in charge—assisted no doubt by the quieter generation which preceded them—folk born in the 1920s and 1930s who hit mid-life in the 1970s and 1980s and many of whom now enjoy retirement. The boomers as a generation have received enormous attention—much of it from themselves. They were, as one writer has put it, "the victory babies after the War, the first Dr. Spock toddlers, the college classes of the 1960s, those who fought in or protested the Vietnam War and forged the counter-culture." They complained mightily about the efforts and constructions of their parents. With them the term "generation gap" took on new meaning. "Trust no one over thirty," some of them said, but soon enough they had turned thirty and, as that saying quickly disappeared, they focused on the "thirty-something" issues: career, family, relationships, and angst over the meaning and purpose in life. Some folk, perhaps a little unkindly, have suggested that the boomers have been so obsessed with themselves that they haven't paid a lot of attention to the fact that a new generation has come and is now coming of age. This generation—born in the mid-1960s through the mid-1980s—are the teens and twenty-somethings of today. This includes you, the college students and recent graduates of today.

Now, as you know well, your generation already has been the subject of much discussion, especially the top-end of it. Commentators through the 1990s spent a lot of time and energy seeking to define the main characteristics of "Generation X," the "post-boomers," the "baby-busters," the "MTV generation," and so on. Their analyses did not always make pretty reading. The top half of this generation got branded with alienation, anomie, apathy, and self-absorption. And that was just for starters! The "older" members of the new generation were alleged to be drifting and unfocused, to be cautious about any commitments, to be fearful and tentative about the future, paralyzed by social problems, and troubled by a peculiar sense of meaninglessness. Some of their woes were attributed to the "broken-home angst" resulting from their childhood coinciding with divorce's "big-bang" in the 1970s and 1980s, but the emphasis in most analyses seemed to be on accusation rather than explanation and understanding.

I cannot speak to the overall validity of this picture. What I can say is that it does not gel well with the members of this generation I have met over the last decade and whom I meet today. Of course I have met and still meet folk who seem adrift personally, spiritually, and professionally. And yet, the picture presented above doesn't equate either with the commitment of many students to their studies and their seriousness about career or with their willingness to serve others both in college and in a year or more of service work beyond it. Nor does the picture reflect the desire of many young adults to live good and moral lives and to shape their lives with an outlook that gives them purpose and meaning. The picture of a rather lost and self-indulgent generation is at odds with my observation of a greater conviction among young men and women that such values as honesty and fidelity are to be treasured and that the temptations to abuse alcohol and drugs and sex are to be resisted.

Now you may wonder where all this generational stuff is leading. Well, I want to say that in a certain sense it is leading nowhere. The reason is this: When it comes to responding to the word of God, generational analysis is of little relevance. The word of God is not spoken only to one generation; nor is it packaged in different ways to different generations. It is plainly spoken across the generations. It is not spoken to groups artificially labeled by their ages; it is spoken to each one of us, regardless of our generation.

We, as disciples across the generations, are all sons and daughters of the one God. We are members of one family and we must live up to the family-likeness, which means living with the all-embracing love God bestows. There isn't a moral code for one generation which differs from another. All of us are challenged to extend compassion and mercy and forgiveness. All of us are called forth to be single-hearted and sincerely devoted to God and neighbor.

But perhaps we can help each other better across the generations to live out our shared calling. We need to bear a responsibility to nourish each other in the faith. Your generation might even have a special role to aid reconciliation among and within the generations which precede yours. We must not be simply shaped by the age in which we live and molded by some externally imposed set of generational expectations or characteristics. We must be leaven within our time and within our generations in spreading the good news and in living our Christian calling.

Generations pass but love endures. Like the Lord Jesus (and in the words of the Australian poet and cartoonist Michael Leunig):

> Let us live in such a way
> That when we die
> Our love will survive
> And continue to grow.

"Lord, are they few in number who will be saved?"

The End Times & Who Will Be Saved

One Monday night I was in my room tapering off after a long and tiring day. I think I was catching the late news when a student came by to see me. He seemed a bit agitated and excited and quickly got to the point. He wanted to know my views on the end times. He was curious about my views on the second-coming, the final judgment, and the end of the world as we know it. He revealed to me that he had read the Book of Revelation twice over a recent break and that he had thought a lot—indeed couldn't stop think-ing—about all this. The approach of the new millennium seemed to have given a particular urgency to his focus on apocalyptic literature.

Now with that "warm-fuzzy" pastoral approach for which I'm renowned after a hard day of work, I told the young man that I didn't really think much about the end times. Furthermore, I strongly implied that he would be better off if he thought less about it as well. But he was not deterred. In fact, he started pressing me on what I had been taught during my seminary formation about the end times and about who would be saved and about the great final battle. He looked at me with something beyond disap-pointment and dismay—perhaps it was even close to dis-dain!—as I explained that I hadn't really dealt with the matter at any special length.

Just for a moment there on that Monday night I wished I knew more and could satisfy better the young man's inquiries. But I dodged his questions further and told him not to worry so much about the end of the world and the final judgment. I instructed him instead simply to lead a good life, to follow Jesus' way, and then the rest would take care of itself whenever the day of final judgment came.

Now normally my inadequate answers to questions don't bother me much, but I felt uneasy about my weak response. And I have to confess that I haven't got much more to add on the whole matter of the end times. We can only continue our efforts to live waiting and in hope for the final coming of Christ and to be prepared whenever that may occur. Yet I do want to focus further on an ancillary question raised by the young man—namely, who can be saved?

Given what we know of our God through Christ Jesus, it seems reasonable to conclude—with 1 Timothy 2:4—that God "wants all to be saved" and is ready to give his grace to all. God isn't in heaven with a big chart on which two teams have already been picked—the saved and the damned—and we are just going through some predeter-mined motions to get into the assigned columns. Rather, each one of us is called to respond to God's self-revelation in Christ and to use the human freedom with which we are endowed to return ultimately to God. This is surely God's hope for each one of us. It is a wonderful and extraordinary call offered not only to some specially qualified group but to all of us, whatever our limitations and weaknesses.

This reassuring view has always been particularly comforting to me. It is as if I know for sure that God is on my side. God is for me and for you. But I occasionally worry that I rest too comfortably in God's promise and so remove the real challenge from responding authentically to God's call. An Australian like myself might describe my complacency as the "don't worry, it'll be right" approach to salvation. This approach seems, to put it mildly, inadequate if one listens to Jesus' response when asked the question: "Lord, are they few in number who will be saved?" He replied: "Try to come in through the narrow door. Many, I tell you, will try to enter and be unable" (Lk 13:23-24).

This is a bit unsettling, don't you think? And yet I like to think there is a definite silver lining in the proverbial dark cloud of this unsettling response. Here the Lord gives us not simply a response to the question asked but an additional answer to another and more important question: How is one to be saved? It would seem we have direct guidance that it is through the narrow door. Scripture scholars have expended lots of energy explaining that there was a narrow gate leading into Jerusalem known as the needle's eye through which a big, richly loaded camel could not fit. Perhaps in light of that we might assume that Jesus was guiding his listeners and us to cut down on our baggage of possessions and privileges.

There is, however, more at work here. Jesus Christ, our Savior, is the narrow door for us. He is the source of our salvation and the guide to it. The Christian message and call is extended to all, but it is not easy. Its meaning is centered on Jesus, the way, the truth, and the life. Amidst the range of options and choices before us, we must with God's grace decide to walk the seemingly narrow road of living inspired by the gospel.

Ultimately, salvation is in the hands of our merciful God. We can't assume that salvation is guaranteed for us or denied to us, but I want to suggest that our focus should not be on that matter. Instead, our focus must be on living a life in response to God's call to us. Our concern should not be on the final days but on this day, not on the end times but the present time.

> "This is my body to be given for you. Do this as a remembrance of me. This cup is the new covenant in my blood, which will be shed for you."

Really Present

The University of Notre Dame possesses a truly magnificent piece of property in Land O'Lakes in northern Wisconsin which is graced with pristine lakes and wonderful woods. Scientific researchers conduct classes there for undergraduate and graduate students. The beautiful place also serves as a marvelous retreat for Holy Cross priests and brothers during the summer months and takes one far away from the interruptions and pressures of the regular academic year.

Not long ago I found myself at Land O'Lakes in the company of Notre Dame's legendary president-emeritus, Fr. Theodore (Ted) Hesburgh. Fr. Ted and I arranged to say Mass for the Notre Dame summer-session students in the rustic little chapel which sits right on the edge of Tenderfoot Lake. It was agreed that I would preside and

34

Fr. Ted would preach at the Mass. After the gospel was read I duly sat down and settled comfortably into my chair as Fr. Ted began to preach. I had a wonderful view out the window of the chapel toward the lake and soon I found my attention diverted by the sheer beauty of it all and also by the antics of a couple of loons. I could hear Fr. Ted speaking of the importance of the eucharist, but it is fair to say that I was not really present to his words.

My attention was quickly refocused, however, when I heard Fr. Ted mention my name. I had one of those "What did he say?" experiences, and discreet inquiries later allowed me to clarify that Fr. Hesburgh had conveyed to his student congregation that of all the services performed by a priest, there could be nothing more important than offering Mass. He had added to this that he was sure that this also was the case for "Fr. Bill." And, indeed it is.

Sometimes when you come to Mass you might find yourself following a path similar to the one I followed that day—you might find your attention drifting off in any number of directions. You have the people in the church or chapel to check out, of course, the inevitable scoping that is rather natural for young men and women. You sometimes have lots of things on your mind—everything from your latest sporting "triumph" to your minor roommate hassle or the project that is due tomorrow morning. On some occasions you carry heavy burdens and your concerns are focused on such difficult news as your parents are separating or that your best friend has been hospitalized. In such circumstances it can be a challenge to be truly present and attentive. The Mass becomes an event we merely attend rather like spectators but in which we hold back from true participation.

To limit our active participation in the eucharist in any way—even inadvertently—is truly a tragedy because in our lack of presence we might miss some aspects of the continuing presence of Christ which is a central reality of our life of faith. Within the church this presence shows itself in various ways, but especially at Mass. There, Christ is present from the beginning in the congregation gathered in his name. He is present in the reading and preaching of the word and in the celebration of the memorial of Christ's death and resurrection. But, most crucially, he is present in an altogether special way when, by the action of the Holy Spirit, bread and wine are changed into his body and blood. As a result, in holy communion, according to the words of the gospel, we eat the flesh of Christ and drink his blood (John 6:53). The appearance remains the same but the inner reality is changed.

The Mass has its origins in the Last Supper which Jesus celebrated with his disciples when he identified himself with the bread and the wine ("This is my body," etc.) and directed his followers to "do this in remembrance of me" (Lk 22:19). In the eucharist, Christ's great act of self-offering on the cross is renewed among us through the gifts of his body and blood. It has been so from the days of the earliest Christian believers down to our own time.

How the elements of bread and wine are transformed into Christ's body and blood remains beyond a normal explanation. It is a mystery of faith. But what is more clear, and abundantly so, is why the change takes place. It is so that through receiving the sacrament we may be changed into being more fully the people of God, the very body of Christ. Christ offers us himself as food and drink for our nourishment. We have communion with Christ himself and through this sacrament receive the richest food for mind and heart and soul. In a direct way we are fed to become more like Christ, to become one with Christ. This is the true food that will give each of us life and give it to us abundantly.

I wish I were able to call loudly and clearly to you who are reading this right now. I want to call you by name so that I would know you are present to me and comprehending what I say. I pray that you will shape your day so that you might attend Mass and be truly nourished at the Lord's table with the essential saving food which will do much more than provide fuel for your body. It is the nourishment that will sustain your life.

"The person
who seeks
God discovers
certain ways
of coming
to know him."

Faith
&
Knowledge

The religious commitments of college students have been the subject of some discussion of late. From the perspective of religious folks there is some good news out there. On campuses at Catholic colleges and at state and private non-religious schools, there is apparently a lot of religious activity going on. Students are seen as more religiously active, prayerful, increasingly generous with their time and talents, and ready to live a moral life.

It is not always easy, of course. In a culture that teaches that one opinion is as good as another, students can be torn between, on the one hand, an intuitive sense (let's call it "conscience") that there are real measures of right and wrong and, on the other, the cultural message that there is no firm basis on which to ground moral teaching or religious conviction. It is simply a matter of what works for each person at the moment. The challenge to make one's way as a Christian in the world is rather daunting when so much of our lives is influenced by the prevailing cultural forces. The messages that bombard us explicitly and implicitly from television and big-selling glossy magazines highlight the attractions of money, sex, and possessions; the usefulness of manipulative skills; the corruptibility of every character; the resort to cynicism and skepticism.

Surprisingly and refreshingly in the midst of this cultural bombardment young Catholics continue to participate in their religious practices, especially the Mass and their personal prayer. They continue their efforts to follow the Christian path. This is something from which to take heart.

But in the midst of this hopeful news there remain what might be called areas for growth. An important one is a concern that many young people, despite their good hearts, don't have a deep or firm grasp on even the essential tenets of their faith. Students are alleged to be unclear about the doctrine of the Trinity, cloudy about the centrality of Christ in salvation history, unaware of the transforming effects of grace, and ignorant of church teaching on both sin and the Christian moral life. The suggestion is made that they don't even know enough to be "cafeteria Catholics," who pick and choose only what they like from the body of Catholic teaching.

Certainly, the argument goes, they don't know enough to appreciate and accept that there is a coherent Catholic vision. This vision which is incarnational and sacramental sees God present and active in our world. The divine presence is found not only within the church through the sacraments and faith communities but in the world at large in a whole variety of events and movements. This vision should serve as a guide for how Catholics live in the world. For example, the notion that each human person is deeply loved by God and gifted with real dignity clearly should make a difference in how we think about abortion, the death penalty, assisted suicide, and euthanasia.

Now it seems that every generation as it gets older loves to talk about the limitations of the succeeding one, and this is happening even now. One senses that some members of my baby-boomer generation are relishing the chance to do a bit of venting. One hears things like, "They don't know the tradition." Or, another favorite is, "They don't know what Vatican II did!" Another popular lament is the one I heard from a colleague (complaining that few students in his class of thirty-five could recite the ten commandments or list the seven sacraments) who asked pointedly, "What did they get from CCD?"

At times I get a bit tired of this criticism. Perhaps I feel some guilt that as a priest I have not been able to do more to assist young men and women to deepen their faith knowledge. Perhaps I recognize the validity in the accusation made about a lot of contemporary preaching that it is comforting pabulum devoid of good catechetical content. Perhaps it is simply that I know of the limitations in my own knowledge of the faith.

However that may be, I want to suggest to you that our life of faith can be enriched by our willingness to deepen our knowledge of it. We can move beyond childish or superficial understandings to grasp more fully the teaching of our church. We don't need to continue to drift along, but rather we can seize opportunities to enliven our understanding of the basis of our faith and the mission of our church.

For some of you, opportunities for this might come if you attend a Catholic college or university. Theology courses should guide you, for example, in reflection on the mystery of the Trinity or on the sacraments. But even for those who have this opportunity, it can sometimes be rather limited and explore just a small part of the broad sweep of Catholic teaching. This might also be the case for those engaged in study groups at Newman Centers or in various campus ministry efforts at other colleges.

What then can one do? I have a suggestion. It is one that provides a good, intelligent person with a wonderful overview of the full range of Catholic teaching in creedal beliefs, the sacraments, the moral life, and prayer. Some of you would be quite familiar with it already and would know that I am referring to the *Catechism of the Catholic Church*. This compendium of Catholic teaching approved by Pope John Paul II and first published in 1994 aims to meet the needs of contemporary Christians like us. It does so well, and we should take full advantage of it. Pope John Paul notes that "in reading the *Catechism of the Catholic Church* we can perceive the wonderful unity of the mystery of God, his saving will, as well as the central place of Jesus Christ, the only-begotten Son of God, sent by the Father, made man in the womb of the Blessed Virgin Mary by the power of the Holy Spirit, to be our Savior. Having died and risen, Christ is always present in the church, especially in the sacraments; he is the source of our faith, the model of Christian conduct, and the Teacher of our prayer."

Despite this endorsement from the pope, when you hear the word "catechism" you might conjure up in your mind vague recollections of folk older than you rambling on about the *Baltimore Catechism* and their rote memorization of its answers to such questions as, "Who made the world?" and so on. Without in any way slighting or disparaging the *Baltimore Catechism*, I want to suggest that the new *Catechism* is a work of a different order. It not only supplies answers regarding our faith, but it serves to deepen and nourish the faith of those who read it well.

The *Catechism* explains that "created in God's image and called to know and love him, the person who seeks God discovers certain ways of coming to know him" (#31). The quest for such knowledge should be central to all of our deepest learning in our college years and beyond. Avail yourselves of this valuable means to know God better and burst the balloons of your would-be critics. And share this fundamental knowledge with others. Don't simply rail like your critics, but put your faith knowledge into practice both now and in the future—especially if in the future you are parents and called upon to serve your children as their first teachers in the faith.

Real Prudence

You might have seen the film *The Graduate*, starring Dustin Hoffman. It was a favorite of college students when I was a student myself, so that was quite a while ago—the late sixties and early seventies. In the film, Dustin Hoffman's character is offered key advice—in fact, just one word. That one word is "plastics." Mr. Robinson (husband of the more well-known Mrs. Robinson played by Anne Bancroft) offers this advice to help the rather aimless Hoffman character secure his future, at least his economic future.

I have a different word which I hope will aid you in securing your future. It is "prudence." This seems to be a kind of old-fashioned word. But what is it really? First let us be clear that prudence is not an attitude of caution, restraint, or timidity. No way! Rather, prudence is essentially the ability to discern what is right. The prudent person is one who can make decisions, and good decisions at that. For example, not driving while drunk, not getting drunk in one of the underage bars in town, not getting drunk at all. But the prudent person does more than act sensibly. At a deep level the prudent person asks: What is the best way for me to do what is right? How can I be what I am truly called to be? Prudence is a gift from God. It is available to all of us.

I think of prudence when I reflect on the story of the Lord's encounter with the rich young man who wanted to know how to share in everlasting life (Mark 10:17-30). I suspect the rich young man had some measure of prudence. He had at least enough that he was seeking to discern the important questions. He knew he had been good in that he had followed all the commandments of the law. And yet there was something that still gnawed away at him, something that wasn't quite right. Within his own conscience he knew it, and this is why he confronted Jesus and why he wasn't satisfied with obeying the commandments as the answer to his question. He knew that observance of the law was not enough.

He sought more, and in response Jesus asked the young man to become a disciple. But there was one condition: he must give up his riches. He was asked to sacrifice the very basis of his security and social status. Called to discipleship, he was forced to confront the reality that it can be costly in terms of worldly things. His response is one of the saddest verses in the gospel, and certainly one of the most human: "At these words the man's face fell. He went away sad, for he had many possessions."

Put yourself in his shoes; imagine yourself—a rich young woman or man of today, a person with a fine education, good job, stylish clothes. People say you "have it all"! How then would you respond? Would you too walk away? Or would you give up everything to follow after Jesus? What would be the prudent thing to do?

Let me suggest that what the young man did was the cautious thing, the restrained thing—yes, the timid thing. But it was not the prudent thing. He left heavy of heart. He left sad because he knew deep within himself that he had refused to be what God called him to be. We are not here to cast stones at the young man, for who among us has really responded fully to what God asks of us? Ask yourself about your own discernment. How have you made major decisions, those choices which set a direction for your life? Are they made out of caution, restraint, timidity? Are you prepared to forego security and status to do what your conscience dictates? Are you prepared to let the call of Jesus operate in your life? Are you even willing to confront Jesus and to ask the question like the rich young man, or do you avoid the call to discipleship or see it in a carefully limited way?

Many of us are engaged with learning, with gaining knowledge. This is a good, and indeed can be a holy, enterprise. But if during our time as students we miss out on the lesson provided by Jesus for the rich young man, then our time has been wasted. It is not enough to be guided just by obedience to the law, important though that may be. We must give of ourselves like Jesus did. We must place the Lord's call above worldly possessions and treasures. The invitation is there: "Come, follow me." We must respond. It's the prudent and the courageous thing to do.

"Put on
the armor
of God
so that you
may be able
to stand firm
against the
tactics of
the devil."

Doing Battle With the Devil

I suspect I'm correct in suggesting that few of us have been required to take up arms and go into battle. We haven't had our physical courage and mettle tested under fire as did many young men of half a century ago. Watching a film like *Saving Private Ryan* might stir some curiosity as to how we might perform in such circumstances, but seeing the film's graphic portrayal of the carnage of war surely leaves most of us profoundly relieved that we have not been called to bear arms and to use them.

Thoughts of battles and struggles come readily and quickly to mind when one is confronted with certain scripture passages such as the Letter to the Ephesians in which those early Christians were instructed to "put on the armor of God so that you may be able to stand firm against the tactics of the devil" (6:10-20). Let me suggest that those stirring words should be taken as instruction for ourselves. Admittedly, some might wince a bit at the explicit military metaphors, but like the Ephesians we are called forth to do battle.

But who exactly are we to engage in this struggle? Over recent decades the imagery of war has been used quite a bit—from the "war on poverty" of the sixties to the "culture wars" of the eighties and nineties. There are lots of "battles" occurring at any time, and we are called to align ourselves with the forces for good in the world engaged in the long struggle with those of evil. Perhaps this injunction to do battle might nudge us to stand more robustly for the culture of life in its gargantuan fight against the many elements that make up the culture of death. Such action would surely be to the good.

A careful reading of the Ephesians passage, however, clarifies that we are called upon to struggle against a distinct foe. We are called not simply to counter flesh-and-blood enemies but the devil himself. We are to stand firm against "the cosmic powers of this present darkness, against the spiritual forces of evil in the heavenly places."

Now this is not the usual foe that "learned" folk—those who study and teach in universities and colleges—of our time readily identify. They are more likely to think of the devil, if at all, as merely a symbol of evil forces and inclinations rather than as a personal spiritual figure. And, I admit to you, I have entertained thoughts which lean in that direction.

My thoughts which largely gutted the devil of any threatening significance to me personally were challenged recently when I found myself in Dublin and listened to a homily by an Irish priest who spoke fervently about the danger of the devil. With real conviction he warned his small and rather elderly congregation of Satan's threat. With a certain dramatic flair he gave counsel as to how to ward off that dangerous foe when he came near to tempt us and to entrap us. He suggested that one place one's hands over one's ears and recite constantly the name of the Lord Jesus—Jesus, Jesus, Jesus! I smiled smugly at his homiletic endeavors and later recounted the story to friends, seeing it as a remnant of the Irish spirituality that had such a claim on James Joyce and company.

Subsequently, however, my prayer and reflection have pulled me up a little, and I find myself chuckling less at this priest's earnest counsel. Instead my thoughts return to a book I read a couple of summers ago by the American scholar Andrew Delbanco. Its title says a lot: *The Death of Satan: How Americans Have Lost the Sense of Evil.* Delbanco notes that Satan may have managed a grand accomplishment in the late stages of the twentieth century by persuading so many "modern" folk, perhaps even some of us, that he doesn't really exist. And, if Satan doesn't exist, we need hardly defend against him or do battle with him. Indeed, we can imagine ourselves as quite capable of dealing with matters and forging our own way without any special reliance on God at all. Once we reach this point we have been entrapped in the crucial inclination to sin which resides in the human desire to act independently of God.

Andrew Delbanco suggests that the Puritans, the first generation of English settlers in North America and intensely religious people, thought that Satan met his greatest success when he seduced believers into imagining that they were without sin. But perhaps today the devil meets as much or even more success by persuading people like us that we don't really need to combat him, that it is old-fashioned or out-of-place to fight the battle and to put on the armor of God.

Brothers and sisters in the Lord, don't succumb to this subtle persuasion, to this temptation from the devil.

Instead put on the belt of truth, protect yourself with the breastplate of justice, and take up the shield of faith in one hand and the sword of the Spirit, the word of God, in the other. Christians have the weapons to fight the devil and the hostile and evil forces today, and we must use them.

Men & Women—
Love & Friendship

"Lord, make me an instrument of thy peace; where there is hatred, let me sow love; where there is doubt, faith; where there is despair, hope; where there is darkness, light; and where there is sadness, joy."

My Friend Francis

An insightful Australian priest, Fr. Edmund Campion, observed in his book *A Place in the City* that "to be a Catholic is to belong to a very large family, some of whom are saints." Catholic devotion to the saints is different from the celebration of heroes and heroines of another time. In the Catholic tradition the saints are not simply figures from the past but still-living contemporaries who pray for us and can serve as our role models. As Fr. Ed notes, "there are saints for every circumstance and season." A patron saint might be a special help and aid one in following better the Christian life. Saint Francis of Assisi has been such a saint for me.

The figure of Francis of Assisi is well known. His way of experiencing God and the shaping of his life on the basis of that experience resulted in a distinctive spirituality which has attracted and inspired numerous Christians and non-Christians alike. I suspect I have been influenced in my attraction to Francis by my brother Phillip, who serves the church as a member of the religious order Francis founded. Yet, I sometimes am a bit perplexed by my attraction to this great saint. Francis had some distrust of human learning, seeing that the puffery it sometimes causes would prove an impediment to truly living for God's sake. And I spend my days working in a university setting as a priest-scholar-teacher engaged in that learning enterprise. I must confess that I've never come across any rousing endorsement by Francis of the particular ministry I undertake. Nonetheless, he has a hold on me.

Francis was the son of a wealthy cloth merchant, but as a young man he became dissatisfied with the extravagant way of life possible to him. His eyes were opened increasingly to the suffering of the poor and maimed around him. He possessed a particular horror of leprosy, but one day when he met a leper he forced himself not only to give him alms but to kiss him. Following this climactic experience Francis rejected wealth, honor, and comfort and positively sought poverty. Later, when praying at the church of San Damiano, he heard the figure on the cross address him: "Francis, repair my church." He initially took the instruction quite literally but gradually came to appreciate that the injunction was to be taken in a much wider sense.

His original conversion was completed, and his vocation took final shape when he heard a priest read from the gospel (Matthew 10:5-14) Jesus' instructions to his disciples when he sent them out to preach. Francis took this as a personal command and acted on it. He lived as he understood the apostles had lived, obeying the gospel himself and calling others to do the same. For a time Francis had been searching for purpose and direction in his life, and he had experienced inner doubt and conflict. Now all the disjointed pieces and fragments of his life fell into place. He experienced an inner freedom and a deep joy in the Lord. Put simply: following his conversion, Francis was filled with God.

Francis' model in his relationship to God was Jesus. For him, God was a loving Father whose fatherhood embraced all creatures, and since each creature was in its own way the image of the Father, each was worthy of reverence. Francis never at any stage lurched into any kind of "New Age" pantheism and identified nature itself with God. He simply affirmed the Genesis credo about the world: "God created it and it was good." The world was a sign, a sacrament of God.

This affirmation of life, of existence, and of creation is a distinguishing feature of Francis' message. God, for him, was not hidden behind the world, nor was the Creator exalted by denigrating his creatures. Francis appreciated that God can never truly be found beyond this world unless one recognizes that God comes into and makes himself known in the world. Seeing God and creation in this way, it was natural that Francis did not flee from the world but loved it without possessiveness. Francis, I hope and pray, has guided me to see better the world in this way.

Once Francis experienced God in his life he was eager to return to the Father who created him. He therefore undertook to follow Christ, for Jesus was the way to the Father. Francis acted on his call to follow Jesus by living in simplicity and poverty and by being of service to others. He approached life in the spirit of a true disciple seeking to imitate the person of Jesus as he saw it in the gospels. Francis' imitation of Jesus finds its fullest manifestation in his practical detachment from self and from material possessions. He was content to possess and be possessed by Christ alone, and the imprinting on his body of the mysterious marks of the stigmata—the same wounds as on the body of the crucified Christ—testify to his success. Francis' very success worries me, however. He reveals how truly one can follow Jesus, but when I look upon his powerful witness I'm troubled by my own sad limitations in this regard.

Francis, however, has not simply served as an "impossible" target for me. He illuminates how I might join him in following the Lord more faithfully. Francis' crucial focus on the importance of poverty especially aids my own attempt to come closer to God. Francis' poverty was not restricted to material poverty, to austerity in the use of things. It went much deeper. Poverty meant complete renunciation of self in the deepest humility. As the theologian Louis Lavelle explained in *Four Saints: The Meaning of Holiness*, poverty means a surrendering to God of "our whole soul, naked and free, devoid of all attachment to anything apart from him." Poverty means hollowing out in the soul a vacant place which has to be enlarged until "nothing remains but free and empty space for God himself to fill." Poverty allows God to dwell within and as such it is the greatest of treasures because it teaches us to renounce all in order to gain all. Francis saw poverty as the way to God, and living in poverty he came to experience God in his abundance.

I have some really good friends whose advice and counsel I value greatly. But rarely have they been able to guide me and challenge me so effectively as my saintly friend Francis. He helps clarify for me what are the most important aspects of life and how I must allow God to dwell within me. You may have your own favorite saints and guides, but if not, let me recommend holy Francis to you. His friendship is truly worth having.

Students & Suffering

Whenever I am asked to reflect on the difficult subject of human suffering, my mind travels quickly back to a letter I received from a friend of mine early on during my years in the seminary. His mother had died about six months before he wrote to me, and he had been constantly at her side during the final months of her painful ordeal with cancer. Her illness and death threw him into a funk—a really dark mood—and he seemed to be drifting along trapped by his grief and suffering. That, at least, is how it seemed to me, and I had written telling him of my love and concern for him but also encouraging him to re-focus and to re-engage his work and so forth.

He replied to me, and I still have the letter he wrote. He responded kindly to my somewhat insensitive words to him and told me how he was doing. In the course of his letter, he addressed the matter of how he and I confronted suffering—at least as he saw it. This is what he wrote:

> Besides, our outlooks on life are diametrically opposed—you still retain a hope for bettering the world, I don't. You see your task as that of alleviating suffering; I see my task as sharing in suffering. I don't believe one is right and the other wrong— both are necessary parts of reality. It just seems to me that whatever we do suffering remains, and just as important as reducing suffering is the ability to understand suffering.

My friend's words left a mark upon me, and I have thought about them over the years since. As my own direct experience and knowledge of suffering has grown during this time, I have come to see that one should not make too much of the distinction between alleviating suffering and sharing in it. The two tend to be related in my experience in ways that are difficult to describe.

Now I cannot tell you that I have endured a lot of suffering. But my life has intersected with those of young men and women who have suffered deeply in ways beyond the normal teenage angst or post-college blues. Rather strangely, one sometimes hears the comment that "students know little of suffering." Of course, this remark is usually uttered by those who don't really know students. They don't know of the young woman trapped by the deep unhappiness of her childhood or of the young woman so psychologically troubled that she destroys her own body. They neither know of the young man whose father was ripped from him by a tragic car accident nor of the young man who hides his grief and pain at the breakup of his parents' marriage behind his guarded and cynical exterior.

In fact all of us know what suffering is to some extent or other. It is unquestionably part of our human condition.

It might result from fissures in our families. It might be shabby treatment from those whose friendship and trust we yearn for. It might involve the fatigue and frustration in our studies and seeing the crumbling of our carefully made academic plans—those painful realizations that we are not going to be doctors or engineers. It might come in being rejected for the nice position or good graduate program on which our heart was set. It might come through the experience of loneliness and homesickness or in observing the pain and distress in the lives of others and being pretty helpless to do much about it. Suffering is part of every life and is to be expected in our own.

What should we do? Suffering can't be explained away. It is too real for that. But could we deny it? Perhaps for a time, but only to our ultimate cost. Should we simply endure it? Perhaps at times the "grin and bear it" approach is all we can muster, but it is hardly the best long-term approach. I want to suggest that in the end we must accept the suffering that comes and use it. This is hard to explain and even harder to do. But we must not let suffering push us to withdraw or let it embitter and harden us. Rather we should see in suffering a means to become more open to the suffering of others. Through experiencing pain ourselves we can become like my dear friend and be much more able to empathize with others and to help them in their need.

My fellow Holy Cross priest, Fr. John Dunne, in his marvelous book *The Church of the Poor Devil*, maintains that "it is willingness to suffer that enables us to love." The suffering can shape and mold us to be more willing to give of ourselves to others not out of some kind of *noblesse oblige* but out of a recognition that we are wayfarers on a common journey who need to support each other along the way. We should take Jesus as our model, the very one who was willing to drink the cup he was poured and given, difficult though that was. We must, with God's help, do the same.

Some years ago I visited a place of sadness and terrible tragedy—the small southeast Asian nation of Cambodia, or

Kampuchea. This country's recent history has been simply horrendous, as you might know. The Vietnam War spilled over its borders and half of the country was bombed by B-52s, causing death, injuries, and great disruption. Then in 1975 Pol Pot and the vicious Khmer Rouge came to power. They began a virtual genocide on the Cambodian people. In acts of dastardly madness they began to kill off teachers and doctors and civil servants—anyone with education. They tried to destroy religion and traditional Cambodian culture. They drove people from the cities to the countryside, and there was mass starvation. In all, over a million people were killed and the whole infrastructure of the country destroyed. Eventually Pol Pot was forced out and has since died. But the country he so brutalized still hobbles along trying to regain some real stability and peace.

During my visit to Cambodia I visited Tuol Sleng prison in Phnom Penh, a horrible torture chamber where ordinary men and women were subjected to unspeakable acts of brutality. I saw Cheong Ek, one of the "killing fields," a site of mass graves containing the remains of literally hundreds of Cambodians. It was very troubling and moving all at once. But the most poignant episode during my stay occurred on a visit to the National School of Music and Dance. There I observed a group of elderly ladies, who somehow or other had survived the horrors of Pol Pot, instructing young girls in traditional Cambodian dance. They were reclaiming and rebuilding their decimated culture in a very tangible way. The sadness and pain of the old ladies was deeply etched in their faces, but it did not prevent them from generously and gently passing on to the eager and happy little girls their treasured knowledge of the beautiful dance which brings such joy and delight to the Cambodian people. On one level it was a small thing. On another I took it as a marvelous sign of the capacity of the human spirit to survive and to struggle on despite ordeals of suffering.

Christians have as their guide and model Jesus, the suffering servant. He knows of our pain and suffering from first-hand experience and walks beside us in our times of distress. His support can help us bear the heaviest of burdens and not be paralyzed by them. Accepting suffering, sharing it, and working to alleviate it are all related aspects of the deep hope that comes from knowing that Jesus is the very one who suffered and died for us.

"You are my friends, if you do what I command you."

Correct Friends

College is a wonderful place for making friends. Lots of folk of the same age are gathered around with similar interests and shared activities. The true friends one makes in college are likely to be friends for life. You will keep in touch even when you move to different parts of the country and commit yourselves to families and careers that increasingly occupy your time.

Building such lasting friendships, the kind that extend far beyond your graduation day, is no easy thing. Too often the relationships forged in college are rather superficial, which is not surprising if they are built primarily around going to bars and drinking. There can be a lack of depth and honesty to them. We can feel unable to truly share important aspects of our lives. At times conversation can seem limited to sport, smart comments about members of the opposite sex, and television shows full of sarcasm and cynicism. Beliefs, values, and commitments get short-changed.

Now I want to add a somewhat old-fashioned word and practice into the discussion of friendship. The word and practice is "correction." Now "correction" probably conjures up for you memories of your childhood or your adolescence when you got caught doing something and your parents decided to take a little action—loss of allowance, grounding, etc. Most of the time we think of correction as a task to be undertaken by someone else. Yet, I want to suggest to you that there is a call for Christian men and women to undertake this practice. Indeed the gospel (Matthew 18:15-20) includes the instruction for disciples that if your brother or sister does wrong, speak to them. Do it alone or with two or three others or with the whole community, but do it. Speak up. Don't keep your mouth shut. Don't acquiesce in wrong and pretend you don't notice. What the gospel implies is that if we are members of a Christian community we won't see correction as somebody else's job. Rather, our vocation is partly fulfilled through the work of brotherly or sisterly correction.

Is this easy to do? I don't think so. For a start, there is little support in the broad culture for such activity. The collapse of shared moral truths in our society seemingly leaves it up to everyone to do what they want. Who can say what is right or what is wrong in any situation? No one should dare impose their morality on anybody else, should they? One fears raising topics of morality for fear of being branded moralistic or preachy.

In addition to the societal moral vacuousness we can have two tendencies which inhibit our capacity to offer genuine correction. The first is to avoid the person in need of correction but to start complaining to others and back-biting. We never confront the person or the situation openly or honestly. The second approach, which is one I've occasionally and unfortunately tried, is to get all worked up and let someone have it with both barrels. Here one uses a few pejorative words without much concern for the consequences. This approach usually develops from anger or frustration. Sadly, it is rarely done to truly aid the person we confront. In fact, it usually aggravates the situation.

How then can we proceed? For one thing, this brotherly or sisterly correction is not about the trivial. This has to be serious stuff and is not a flippant activity. It is not a license for busybodies or narks. We have to be concerned with aspects of a person's life which lead them to drift from responsible and generous Christian living. It might mean calling someone when they get behind the driver's wheel drunk because they endanger their own life and those of others, or objecting when our friends target someone for ridicule or abuse. It might mean confronting brothers or sisters who wrap themselves in selfishness and focus only on themselves at the expense of others, especially those who use others without care or commitment. Very importantly, it means challenging those who seem to be squandering the gifts and opportunities they have received from God. Real friendship involves encouraging each other to develop further the talents we possess. It also means supporting each other in the daily endeavor to live our lives with integrity. True friends are willing to confront, to challenge, and to call forth the best from those for whom they care.

Now, I have spoken mainly about mustering up our courage to call a brother or a sister to task. But we must acknowledge that there is another side of the story. We may be the ones being called! This is where it really gets tough. Who likes to be challenged or corrected? Not me, I can assure you. But if we see it is done with love, if it is the work of a true friend, then I suspect we will know that genuine challenge and correction—the sort that develops from true friendship—brings not only a chastening and a redirection in life but also a deepening of friendships and a powerful joy that is mutual. It is like everything else Jesus touches.

The Lord gives us his friendship (John 15:14-15) and asks us to follow his lead. Those whom Jesus has chosen to be his friends cannot help feeling bound by his example in their authentic relations with one another. He it is who ultimately calls us to be real friends, even correct friends.

> "It is God's will that you grow in holiness; that you abstain from immorality, each of you guarding your body in sanctity and honor."

St. Valentine's Letter on Love & Sex

You may wonder if a priest could have much to say regarding St. Valentine's Day. But let me remind you that according to legend, the Valentine takes its name from a young priest who lived in ancient Rome. He was imprisoned for his faith. He wanted to assure his loved ones of his well-being and of his love for them. Hence his messages, carried by a friendly dove: "Remember your Valentine" and simply, "I love you." Thus did the Valentine have its beginning. It's not exactly Romeo and Juliet, is it?

Anyway, I confess I'm no longer a young priest, but I want to offer a

St. Valentine's Day message of a sort to suggest that women and men are called to establish and develop authentic friendships. Such friendships allow us to know each other as distinct individuals and not as stereotypes or objects. Such friendship provides the basis for any lasting relationship.

Now let me move beyond this simple but important call and speak of our lives as sexual beings. One might say that contemporary society has come a long way since the so-called "sexual revolution" of the 1960s and 1970s. This revolution promised "liberation" from societal restraints of days of old. One need only look to what characterizes portrayals of sex today to see that this "revolution" certainly brought significant changes. There is endless pushing of sex and sexual imagery in society. Casual sex, indeed promiscuous sex, is seemingly endorsed by the culture, by television and film and advertising—Calvin Klein, and all that. The sexual activity message is delivered week after week on the networks, and sex is presented as more or less a recreational activity. It all looks like so much fun, doesn't it? The beautiful young actors and actresses rarely face consequences for their sexual indulgence. There is little evidence of sexually transmitted diseases, AIDS, abortion, or illegitimacy. There is not much mention either of sex without love that is dispiriting or of the fearful, tentative quality of many contemporary relationships and of marriages that don't last. No. Sex is presented in a rather hedonistic way as just fun.

Those with eyes to see and ears to hear—even priests—know that sex without love and vowed commitment occurs almost everywhere. Sadly, more often than not, alcohol plays a part in this. Sometimes I hear of the aftermath of a sexual encounter from folks who think again about their actions. I hear from those who clearly have been used. They are confused, angry, and often filled with a kind of self-loathing at being so easily exploited. They feel somewhat deceived by the culture's promise of instant gratification. Some, at least, gain clarity that gratification and deep fulfillment are two quite different realities.

During college it seems casual sexual relations can easily become exploitation, for these years are so filled with options and transitions that even the most sincere romantic commitments of the "Oh, but we're different, we really love each other" type are frequently broken. In the midst of all the societal pressures and the endless sexual imagery I want to put before you the challenge to live a chaste life and to encourage those of you who do so at present to continue on this path.

"Chastity" sounds like an old-fashioned word, but it is really a timeless word appropriate for any age. It implies, as the insightful Mary Patricia Barth Fourqurean explains, that "we will not say more with our bodies than we mean in our hearts." It means sincerity. It means sincere "love for God, for others, for ourselves." In marriage, as Fourqurean notes, "chastity does not mean sexlessness but rather faithfulness." It means "fidelity," a word we need to use and to practice more. In "singleness" chastity involves refraining from pre-marital sex. It does not mean obsessive scrupulosity about sex. Rather, chastity calls us not to follow the path of indulgence but to seek the truly good life where deep commitment, genuine integrity, and true love can be fully expressed between one man and one woman as husband and wife.

Let me not suggest that this is easy; it is not. And yet, with God's grace, we are capable of living and loving in this way. It can call forth our courage and virtue and preserve our true beauty, dignity, and self-respect. Well, perhaps I've gone on a bit long. St. Valentine's messages were shorter, I guess! But believe me, this rather longer message comes to you out of love.

"Love and honor each other as husband and wife for the rest of your lives."

Men, Women, & Marriage

I recently was surprised to learn that the incidence of divorce among people in their twenties reached record highs during the past decade. Almost forty percent of all divorces in the United States occurred to couples under thirty. I had shared a rather widespread perception of divorce as a midlife phenomenon. My assumption was that divorce came primarily either when a middle-aged couple saw their children leave home and found difficulties in maintaining their relationship, or as a result of the phenomenon of the middle-aged man dispensing with the mother of his children to take on his arm the so-called trophy wife. Yet, the twenties are the most likely time to get divorced.

The social scientists and the marriage therapists have plenty of explanations for this occurrence. They suggest that there is a general societal difficulty with commitment and permanency—jobs are no longer for life, objects are disposable and so, it seems, are relationships. Among the more specific causes they offer are changing marital roles and increased expectations of the partners, the passage of no-fault divorce laws and the greater social acceptability of divorce, unrealistic ideas about marriage, poor communication skills, and what some describe as greater narcissism among young adults. These have all contributed to the increase in early marital breakups. Young, recently divorced folk offer comments to explain their situation, like:

"It was a real mistake to marry so young. I didn't understand we had very different values and backgrounds."

or "The reasons for my divorce were simple—we were both very young, and we had no idea what marriage was."

or "You realize that there are more ingredients in a marriage than thinking you're in love."

Concern at the rising rate of divorce among young people has helped launch the "marriage movement," which wants to emphasize training for marriage in hopes of lowering the divorce rate of the generation which will marry in the next decade. State legislatures, such as Florida's, now pass laws requiring high school students to be taught marital and relationship skills. I hope such measures will be of help.

In light of the situation suggested by such laws and the high divorce rate that stands behind them, it might be appropriate to give a little thought to marriage. Believe it or not, you will probably get married; and it's helpful to think of what it involves before you start walking up the aisle. I want to offer just three thoughts, but before doing so let me provide the disclaimer that I have never been married and don't expect to be married. I cannot speak from direct experience, and I encourage you to broach the topic in a serious way with those who can. Nonetheless, I hope you won't tune me out.

The first point is that we reaffirm our robust faith in the institution of marriage. We must do this, despite the sheer disposability of some contemporary marriages and despite the skepticism that wedding vows have lost their credibility. Surely there is something profound in God's word as recorded in Genesis: "It is not good for one to be alone." Man and woman were created for each other. In their single divine origin lies the basis for the Genesis teaching about marriage: "That is why a man leaves his father and mother and clings to his wife, and the two of them become one body" (Gn 2:24). They give to each other and become one as husband and wife. This is as it should be not only in the past but now and into the future.

My second point is to affirm the essential equality of woman and man. In the book of Genesis, Yahweh God is depicted as a matchmaker for Adam. Mismatched at first with animals and birds, none of whom proved a suitable partner, Adam at last found his equal in his female counterpart whom God formed not from mere clay but from the very substance of Adam. Both male and female are equally marvelous parts of God's creation.

While woman and man are truly equal, the Lord made them and their descendants fascinatingly different, not only biologically but also in other ways. Of course, there are all kinds of stereotypes of what is male and what is female. Some would argue that men are likely to be more aggressive and competitive, that they deal more easily with generalities and ignore details, that they reason logically and objectively, that they keep their feelings inside, and that they will never ask directions when lost. In turn, it is said that women are more likely to be cooperative and caring, to be disposed to love, to be concerned with details, to think intuitively, and to show feelings with ease. Critics of such categorizations argue that these are just artificial images putting pressure on every man and every woman to conform and act in a certain way. Perhaps so. Who can dispute that we are all distinct individuals and that socialization plays its part in who we are? That conceded, however, I would suggest that it is a valuable use of one's college and post-college years to deepen your appreciation of the different qualities and experiences of men and women. Male-female encounters should be much more than a series of skirmishes in the never-ending battle of the sexes. We need to talk about our different approaches and outlooks, and even laugh about them. This will help us learn about and understand each other better. The real equality which our Creator ordained can be best experienced when enlivened by such understanding.

My third point is very simple. Mean what you say when you commit yourself in the marriage ceremony to "love and honor each other as husband and wife for the rest of your lives." Mean this holy promise knowing full well that marriage is neither easy nor safe. It's a step into the dark and you cannot predict what will happen. Naturally, it makes sense to get to know the person with whom you plan to set out on this journey and to do this before you depart—not midway through it. And don't pretend that you can do this well by living together before your marriage—the well-worn, "let's do this on a trial basis first" rationalization. Couples who live together before marriage actually have a significantly greater chance of divorce than those who do not. Take advantage of the marriage preparation programs offered by the church. Couples are regularly surprised by how helpful they are in furthering good communication. Such programs can help prepare you to commit yourself to your spouse irrevocably knowing well that while there will be times of joy and successes, there will be sorrows and disappointments. Keep in mind that no one human being can in any full and complete way fill another's desire to be loved. In the end such love can only come from God.

Friends, marriage is not a single event. It is not something you will do on your wedding day, but on that day and every day thereafter. It must be seen as a true vocation, a holy calling. You and your spouse must help each other to live Christian lives, to share your love with others, especially your children, and to root your lives and love in the great love God extends to us.

Women Who Have It All

"There are no more distinctions between Jew and Greek, slave and free, male and female, but all of you are one in Christ Jesus."

"**W**hat do women want?" is a familiar question asked by Sigmund Freud. It is a question that in its essentials has been asked often by men both before and after Freud. These days the question is still asked, but now primarily by women. Men who possess even a modicum of circumspection tend to tread warily around the topic for fear of succumbing to "foot-in-mouth disease" and causing offense. Ultimately, of course, it is women who must wrestle with the issue of what they need to find fulfillment in their lives. Many struggle to choose among work, career, love, marriage and motherhood, etc. Others optimistically hope to "have it all," as the expression goes.

The role of women in American society has been transformed since the 1960s. The publication of Betty Friedan's book *The Feminine Mystique* in 1963 is usually credited with launching the modern women's movement. This work attacked the ideology of domesticity and femininity that allegedly characterized the lives of married women in the 1950s. Friedan sought to "liberate" women from confinement in their homes where they were dependent and unable to express themselves fully.

Whatever the accuracy of this social diagnosis, women, spurred by various economic and personal motives, certainly responded quickly to the call to move beyond the home. Where in 1960 only nineteen percent of women with children under six worked, by 1980 this figure had reached close to fifty percent. Women seized new educational opportunities with alacrity and entered a much wider range of careers—medicine, law, business, journalism, and so forth—which traditionally had been dominated by men. By the nineties the situation differed greatly from that of a quarter century before. Of course, some problems remain— the glass ceiling, inequalities in compensation, subtle forms of sex discrimination such as the perception that women are too empathetic and not sufficiently decisive—but women today have career possibilities that are basically the same as men's.

This focus on work and career in turn has presented new issues and challenges for women. Today's women know these well, and speak of them broadly as the work-life balance. They ask where marriage and family fit into the career possibilities now open to them. The solutions are not readily apparent. Some women, especially professionals and managers, decide to delay marriage and, more notably, to delay pregnancies until they are in their thirties. In other cases, women attempt to be the "supermom" who does it all, juggling work and family life. (Of course, for single mothers this is less of a choice than a necessity.)

Other women who choose to stay at home with their children can experience regret and then worry about the consequences for their careers. Some feel guilt that they are "wasting" their education.

In these new circumstances women worry more about some of the negative aspects of their career/lifestyle decisions—e.g., anxiety and exhaustion, the limits of "quality time," and the quality of daycare as they raise their children. Many contemporary women, it seems, now work harder than did their mothers in performing their particular balancing act. And the satisfactions of work and career have hardly outweighed deeply felt needs for love and motherhood and family. The contemporary woman certainly has found no simple path to happiness and fulfillment.

The anxieties and insecurities of modern women and their readiness to seek advice and counsel has led to the continued amazing success of mass-circulation women's magazines. Throughout the postwar era these periodicals have presumed to instruct women on their appearance and values and given all kinds of advice while always exploiting the woman's role as consumer through their hundreds of pages of advertising. Such glossy publications— *Glamour, Cosmopolitan, Marie Claire,* etc.—continue to fill the shelves of newsstands and find their ways into the hands of millions of intelligent young women. The counsel and advice they offer contemporary women, however, seems decidedly shallow. Increasingly (and surprisingly) the advice is focused on attracting and keeping the attention of men. What else is one to make of articles entitled: "How Do Men See You?"; "Sex Appeal: Do You Know Who He Finds Attractive?"; "Men, Sex and You"; and "What Men Think About Your Look." Such articles cannot simply be dismissed as frivolous, for they have an impact on how many women want to look and on how they act. These magazines supposedly written for women ironically place additional pressures on many young women to please men.

Of course most young women are not solely dependent on women's magazines for advice. They have the rich benefit of good mother-daughter relationships, despite occasional tensions and disagreements. They enjoy the support of women friends, colleagues, and mentors. Nonetheless, I am occasionally struck by the number of intelligent, creative, and thoughtful women who worry about how they will navigate their way forward and get the balance right for themselves and those they love or will love.

Perhaps they should worry less and simply accept that there is no clear road-map toward true fulfillment as a woman that suits all times and situations. No doubt the "answer" to the work-life question might vary considerably for different women and also might vary considerably for the same woman at different stages of her life. A readiness to respect the diverse choices of women seems essential. They should not have to worry about disguising the attractions of motherhood even as they make their way up the corporate ladder. They should appreciate the opportunities before them to fashion their course, knowing full well that this possibility is not one shared by a majority of the world's women who experience more troubling environments where the female fetus is much more likely to be aborted than the male, and where female infanticide, dowry deaths, genital mutilation, and commercial sexual exploitation are all-too-common afflictions.

Well, you may ask, where is all this leading? In a sense it sets a context for my suggestion to female students and recent graduates that as they plot their life path they should keep faith firmly at the center of their reflection and decisions.

I am often moved deeply by the rich faith of the women students and former students whom I know. They inspire me with their ready acknowledgment of Jesus Christ as Lord and Savior. They see how Jesus related to women of his time in extraordinary ways. He was one who broke down barriers and proclaimed a gospel of true liberation; who deemed it an honor to have his feet kissed and washed by Mary, the public sinner; who made the woman at the well of Samaria an apostle to teach her own people that the giver of life was in their very midst. The risen Christ appeared first to a woman, Mary, and entrusted to her the task of bringing the message of his resurrection to the other apostles—and this at a time when women were not accepted as public witnesses.

Women have played a crucial role in proclaiming the good news of the resurrection from that time until our own. They have served as powerful witnesses of obedience and fidelity to the word of God. Even in a patriarchal church and across cultures where men have dominated the public sphere, women have constantly embraced the task of witnessing to Christ. Their contributions have been vast, beginning of course with Mary, the Mother of God, who played such a decisive role in the plan of redemption. Mary Magdalene and Martha in one age, Teresa of Avila and Catherine of Siena in another, on up to Edith Stein and Dorothy Day in our own century—we could easily construct a lengthy litany of holy women. Accompanying them are the countless millions of faith-filled women who have spread the gospel primarily in their families and communities through their loving words and generous deeds. The church has been sustained by them and it still is.

My prayer is that this will continue to be so into the future, whatever the ambivalence that might exist among some young Catholic women about their role in the church—an ambivalence generated by the issue of ordination to the ministerial priesthood, the perception that women's voices are not heard well in church deliberations, and the belief that women should exercise greater roles of leadership and authority in the church. My prayer is offered not simply for the good of the church which so needs the marvelous gifts which women bring to worship and service and which is so impoverished when they absent themselves; it is offered also for young women because it is within the church, even with all its human imperfections, that they can be their best selves. The quest for equality and freedom and true dignity is best pursued in light of the faith that is shared by women and men. All of us ultimately are "one in Christ Jesus" (Gal 3:28). This is the faith that provides real meaning and purpose, provides a reservoir of strength and a barrier against fear, and leads to fullness of life.

Women who really want to have it all don't turn from the practice of their faith. Quite the opposite! They appreciate, as do their brothers-in-Christ, that the absolute fulfillment of their desires is not possible in this world. They don't allow a fruitless quest to "have it all" in personal and material terms to distract them from the profound truth that only when we are subsumed in God's love in eternity will we experience ultimate fulfillment.

> "Be on your guard, stand firm in the faith, and act like men. In a word, be strong. Do everything with love."

True Men

Young males from eighteen to thirty are a key target for television producers. Apparently, advertisers will pay huge sums of money for commercials during shows that gain an audience of such young men. They are consumers with money to spend and who have not established firm brand loyalties. The effort to attract this group of viewers explains such shows like *South Park* and the phenomenon of the "shockumentary." A recent article in the *New York Times* tracked some of the most popular shows for young males according to the Nielsen ratings. This poll came up with such programs as *Whose Line Is It Anyway?* and the *World's Wildest Police Videos* as well as *Monday Night Football* and *World Championship Wrestling*. Of course, the standards like *The Simpsons* and *The X-Files* also rated a mention, but there is a sense that successful shows must appeal to a pretty low common denominator and include some graphic violence or titillation or coarse humor (Homer Simpson can usually be relied upon for the latter!).

Now I don't want to draw too many conclusions from the existence of these programs, just as I wouldn't draw too many from the fact that some young college women watch their favorite soap opera each afternoon. Guys have the right and maybe even the need to hang out occasionally with their friends and watch some low-brow entertainment and engage in a bit of ribald humor. Laughing at Homer Simpson's belching or mooning is not going to end civilization as we know it. Yet the TV producers' pitch for the young male audience at this rather low level does raise some questions. It raises for me questions about what is put before young men and why, what is important to young men and how they clarify what it is that matters, and ultimately what it means to be a man.

One of the reasons I loved the movie *Saving Private Ryan* is that it portrayed without apology a group of men—ordinary men with human limitations—as capable of bravery, virtue, sacrifice, duty, and heroism. Such celebrations of manhood, if you will, have become increasingly rare on the American screen. Men have been portrayed increasingly as immature, manipulative, and cruel, or as weak and superfluous. Suggestions are made that such portrayals reflect reality. Certainly in a broader sense masculinity has become more eviscerated and increasingly stripped of connotations of strength and goodness.

Men, it seems, are a bit lost as to how to behave today, and there is increasing concern about them. The concern derives partly from a review of raw statistics which reveal that men suffer from far higher rates of teenage and adult suicide than women, as well as homelessness, unemployment, homicide, imprisonment, drug and alcohol addiction, heart disease, and a variety of other health problems. The concern also develops out of the seeming lack of clarity about a man's role since the rise of the women's movement. A burgeoning "men's movement" aims to address the alienation and frustration afflicting many of today's men.

Certainly men are not lost for counsel and advice on how to address their situation. A decade ago we had the poet Robert Bly's bestselling *Iron John*, which prompted significant numbers of men to attend wilderness retreats to discover the mythic dimensions of their masculinity. Reports of men beating on drums out in the woods got quite a few laughs and tended to overwhelm Bly's point that young men had become "soft" and had missed out on being initiated into an adult manhood where responsibility, leadership, and protection of the weak are valued. Bly wanted to fill the vacuum that had left young men without proper male parenting or adequate role models.

Another and more explicitly Christian response to the perceived needs of men came in the nineties through Promise Keepers, the movement launched by the former Colorado football coach Bill McCartney. This movement called men forth to honor Christ by loving their wives and children and building up their churches and communities. The movement tended toward a more theologically and politically conservative line. It took some flack for its support for male "headship" of the household, although the movement emphasized equally strongly Saint Paul's call for men to love their wives just as Christ loved the church, which hardly seemed a recipe for male superiority. This surprisingly interracial movement which brought thousands to rallies in football stadiums to hear what was termed "The Gospel of Guyhood" continues its work, but with a lower public profile.

Whatever the impact of Robert Bly or Promise Keepers, I think it fair to say that we are still working today to come to better grips with what it is to be a man. Regrettably, American campuses have not supplied lots of good answers. Guys arrive at college for the most part having just separated themselves from parental control and eager to establish themselves. During their college years, if they are normal, their hormones are raging and they have within them a lot of competitive and even aggressive and combustible energy. How should it be invested and developed?

Let me say first how it shouldn't be treated. It certainly shouldn't be denied or repressed. College is not the place to try to turn men into something they are not. The college experience should not be one giant exercise in a weird kind of "sensitivity training" designed to produce overly-sensitive males. Nor, however, is college the place where young men should give a twisted vent to the powerful and sometimes dangerous energies within them. It is not a place where male camaraderie should degenerate into a suffocating pack mentality which aspires to no higher ambition than getting through classes without much work, getting "blitzed" regularly, getting "laid" whenever the opportunity presents itself, and ripping on those who don't do likewise. College "guys" who follow this path are destined to never really grow up, nor to gain the moral awareness and concern for others that every true man possesses.

If a young male is to become a man, he must choose a path different from either of these. I know it to be possible because I have seen good men emerge during their student years. They do it in much the same way as men have through time, neither by surrendering their masculinity nor by wallowing in a self-centered adolescence, but by undertaking some variation of the journey that all men must make if they are to become their best selves. As the Jesuit scholar Patrick Arnold (who borrows from Joseph Campbell) has observed, the journey involves "leaving the safe comforts of home for an adventurous exploration of the world—and the self. It demands an ordeal—a struggle with demons and dragons real and imagined. And it requires, finally, a return—to a life of service and responsibility." Ultimately, it means discovering how one finds one's true and best self by discerning how one must live for others.

College is the arena where many American men undertake this journey or refuse to face it. You know only too well of the "demons and dragons" that lie in wait for you during your college years, although they are more subtle than fighting either wild beasts or ugly monsters as in classic tales. One's college years are the venue where men emerge by taking on challenges and actions that build and strengthen in them real character more lasting and strong than any muscles built by constant working-out. These are the key exercises a man practices until they become part of his being—telling the truth, discerning what is right and courageously doing it, standing up for the weaker ones, going to the aid of those in need.

True men still possess competitiveness and a hungry energy to achieve when they leave college, but they are well on their way to having much more. They have learned or are well-advanced in learning, as Patrick Arnold has observed, about quiet strength rather than bravado, about making commitments and keeping their word, about thinking for themselves and standing up for principles, about a willingness to fight on behalf of the weak or ignored, and crucially about respecting women. These are not necessarily "lessons" one will obtain in the classroom on your average college campus. So they must be part of your own learning process. Your best teachers may not always be your professors but will be those men who exhibit these qualities. Seek them out and hang around them. Manhood is learned best experientially in the living of it.

To live the Christian life well males must be true men who have moved beyond the base satisfaction of their own desires. They must be strong and loving and "firm in the faith" (1 Cor 16:13-14). Christian manhood is all about heroic self-giving in order to provide for those who will depend on you—your own family, your community, your church, your society. So I say to the male college students and recent graduates who read this to be courageous on the journey. I say to you with heartfelt sentiment, be a man!

> "Let the little children come to me; do not stop them."

Parents of the Future

The prospect of being a parent may not be one to which you pay a lot of attention at the moment. Looking ahead to holding your own child in your arms might not rank as high among your present concerns as getting a date for Saturday. You may not be expending any thought at all on what kind of mother or father you would be. A quite thoughtful junior once told me bluntly, "I'll cross that bridge when I come to it," when I asked him what sort of father he hoped to be. It's not hard to readily sympathize with his view. Nonetheless, being a parent will be among your most important commitments in this life. You will have the sheer joy of bringing forth new life and the great responsibility of helping to nurture and shape another person, your own child. What kind of parent will you be?

This is a question worth asking at this time when American family life has been subjected to significant restructuring and when the stability of family life has suffered a dramatic decline. You would, of course, be well aware of the latter, if not from first-hand experience then from the various articles on the subject and the endless streams of statistics which pour forth. The latter reveal that the divorce rate has tripled over the last thirty years, as has the percentage of children living with one parent. In fact, an estimated forty percent of people now in their twenties—undoubtedly some of you—are children of divorce. Even more of this twenty-something group were latch-key kids, the first to experience fully the downside of the two-income family which is now deemed so necessary to maintain current living standards.

No doubt we could all give examples of the painful reality of pressure on families today. And who couldn't point to cases of family break-up or family tension? Few among us have not witnessed some of this either in our own immediate and extended families or among those of our friends. The circumstances are usually more complex than is revealed by a recitation of statistics. But the picture on both the macro and micro levels warrants prayerful consideration.

What kind of parent will you be? Will your kids be latch-key kids or lonely kids because you have a career and social roles to play, as does your spouse, and you can't provide either quality or quantity time for them? Will you shower your kids with flashy toys and new clothes in a guilty, misguided attempt to demonstrate your love? Will you give them the warmth, the affection, the love which they truly need for their own well-being? Will you be with them to watch them grow?

Now rest assured I'm not going to try to provide a parent's manual here. I readily admit to the challenges involved. Being a parent these days has been described as "like riding a bicycle on a bumpy road—learning to keep your balance while zooming full speed ahead, veering around as many potholes as possible." And one must concede that all child-rearing contains elements of uncertainty and mystery.

All that said, I want to offer a couple of plain thoughts on parenting which might aid your reflection about this life commitment. Might I first suggest simply that you appreciate well that the crucial point of family life is to raise children well. They are not there for you. You are there for them. Good parents know all about personal sacrifice and the delay of certain plans and desires of their own. In reflecting on this I trust you will be able to appreciate better what your parents have done and been for you and to deepen your gratitude to them.

Second, I hope that you will see that your responsibility as parents will extend beyond supplying your children with the emotional care and intellectual stimulation which all the parent manuals recommend. I hope you will see your task as being to steer your children on a moral course and to give them an ethical framework so crucial to healthy life. Related to this, but even more crucial, I hope you will take seriously Jesus' call to "let the little children come to me" (Mk 10:14). Your children must know they are loved by God. The baptism rite suggests that the parents will be "the first teachers of their child in the ways of faith" and asks that they be "the best of teachers" by what they say and do. You must keep the flame of faith alight in the hearts of your future sons and daughters.

A special word to the potential fathers who read these pages. You know well that the father's role has changed significantly over recent decades. The distant and detached father who reportedly consigned the raising of the children to his wife is a relic of another age. Women, of course, still carry and bear the babies, and they are physically equipped—so to speak—to feed them. This reality, in my view, always gives the mother a privileged bond with her child. Mothers simply have natural gifts for nurturing which we should celebrate and not deny in a quest for sameness. But dads must be an integral part of the raising of their own kids. Parenting is best done as a joint project. Too many children have missed their father's presence and love already. Your kids should not be among them. Don't have them say in the future: "Dad was never around for me." Be there every step of the way as protector and guide.

I say to you, Christian fathers-to-be and mothers-to-be, see the majesty of your call to bring new life into this world and recognize that you will be living out your discipleship as you expend the sacrifice and sheer hard work involved in being a good parent. I pray that you will see your parental vocation as linked to that of the Good Shepherd who cares so much for us. Give your children life to the full, keep them safe, and never abandon them.

Mission & Service in the Church & the World

"You must
never be
content to
leave the
poor the
crumbs from
the feast."

Solidarity Forever

Statistics strike many people as boring. They never seem able to convey a meaning that engages people intellectually or grips them emotionally. For example, when we learn that about fifteen percent of the world's population, living mainly in affluent western nations like ours, uses about eighty-five percent of the world's food and other resources, who among us is spurred to undertake any significant action? "What can I do about it?" we ask, or maybe even "So what?" And, of course, the figures soon pass from our minds and again we can focus on our own concerns leaving aside this situation of gross inequality.

Similarly, who among us expends much thought on statistics which reveal the increasing inequality of income and wealth in our economy?

Perhaps there are a few social workers and left-wing economists who raise the matter. Their objections that the rich are getting ever richer and that the gap between rich and poor is widening get lost in the celebration over the indisputable accomplishments of the American economy during the past decade—low inflation and unemployment, budget surpluses rather than deficits, a booming stock market. We all bow down before the Dow-Jones index and luxuriate in the return on our personal investments. We all want to do well while the going is good. In such circumstances there are few persuasive voices raised to challenge the stark inequities of the prevailing system of global capitalism.

I wonder what Jesus would make of our current circumstances. He was not given to quoting statistics and didn't offer a detailed blueprint for a just economic system. He preferred stories to statistics and seemed more eager to change hearts rather than to design systems. But his stories still resound with telling power today.

Consider the parable of Lazarus and the rich man from the Gospel of Luke (16:19-31). We have no difficulty picturing the graphic scene and being moved by it. The rich man, dressed in his fine clothes, feasts every day. Outside his gate lies a beggar longing just to eat the scraps from his table while the dogs lick this poor man's sores. As far as we can tell the rich man didn't do any really interesting sinning. He merely sat back and enjoyed his riches in total indifference to the plight of the poor man. When he died—perhaps as a consequence of his overeating—the unnamed rich man went to a place of torment, in contrast to Lazarus, who found consolation at the bosom of Abraham.

This powerful parable is an unsettling one for all of us. We can identify all too easily with the rich man. We don't take from the poor; indeed, we might even provide some limited assistance to needy folk. But for the most part, we turn a blind eye to the ravages of poverty and inequality at home and abroad. These are matters too "big" for us to attend to. What could our efforts accomplish?

Such excuses for inaction and defeatist rationalizations run counter to the message of Jesus. And they contradict the impassioned call of our church in recent decades for us to work to create a more just social order. Over thirty years ago at the Second Vatican Council the bishops from around the world observed that "God intended the earth and all it contains for the use of every human being and people" (*Gaudium et Spes*, paragraph 69). Everyone, they explained, has a right to a share of earthly goods to ensure their dignity as persons. Building on the teaching of the council, Popes Paul VI and John Paul II strengthened the emphasis on equality. The thrust of their teaching is that Catholics must work as a matter of justice to bring about material conditions where all share in a fully human life, where all share in the world's abundance.

Some commentators find it both surprising and ironic that Pope John Paul II, who did more than any other individual to bring about the collapse of Marxism, is so forceful in his criticism of unbridled free-market capitalism. Their surprise, however, is largely a function of ignorance of the body of Catholic social teaching that places fundamental importance on the dignity of every person, on the call to human solidarity, and on concern for the common good.

Pope John Paul's teaching is rooted in his duty to evangelize and to call attention to the need for policies and programs to check the abuses of the capitalist system. In his visit to North America in 1999 he called upon "international institutions, national governments and the centers controlling the world economy, [to] undertake brave plans and projects to insure a more just sharing of the goods of the world." He asked that attention be paid to such issues as Third World debt relief, foreign economic assistance, and income redistribution. His words are a call to action.

On our campuses we are not in a position to make decisions for national governments or institutions like the IMF or the World Bank. Yet the vision and call of the pope which is rooted in Jesus' teaching must inspire and guide our actions. We must be willing to sacrifice for the sake of including others in the life we enjoy. We, among the "haves," must close the gap which divides us from the "have-nots." We should do this not out of charity but because it is just and good. We must be prepared not only to accept but to advocate and implement a meaningful reallocation of wealth and resources among groups within this country and between this enormously wealthy nation and poorer nations.

Such actions cannot be sustained and executed well simply out of the motivation of kind sentiment and Christian conviction, no matter how deep and well-meaning. Good intentions are not enough. They can even inspire lousy policies as revealed by the failure of certain foreign aid and domestic welfare measures. The Christian vision which the pope presents requires skillful and able implementation. Here is where those at college and in graduate school must accept the challenge, especially those who study economics and business. As you learn about trade, aid, finance, investment, etc., aim not simply to learn the system as it is but how you can modify the prevailing system to better respect each person, especially those who are poor.

Too few students today are truly ambitious in their studies. They prepare themselves too narrowly in order to fill some specific role in the "system." They don't prepare themselves to amend, ameliorate, or transform it. They don't ask enough of those tough questions as to why the statistics are as they are and how they might be changed.

Taking seriously Catholic social teaching and asking these questions is an important responsibility for Catholic students whether they be liberal or conservative, whether they plan to work in the private or the public sector. The university where I teach says in its mission statement that it aims "to create [in its students] a sense of human solidarity and concern for the common good that will bear fruit as learning becomes service to justice." Colleges and universities can play a part in fostering this learning, but ultimately only the students and recent graduates can bring it to fruition. When they do so, young Catholic adults in a profound sense use their education for others and march in solidarity with the poor. Marching this way will mean we will do more than write a check when we see bloated bellies in some foreign country on the network news and more than contribute readily at the food pantry of our local parish. Pope John Paul puts it plainly to each of us: "You must never be content to leave the poor the crumbs from the feast. You must take of your substance, and not just of your abundance in order to help them." This is a vision worth fighting for. Its realization will bring us true solidarity forever.

Work

"Man, created in the image of God, shares by his work in the activity of the creator."

During my years in seminary formation I took a course in which the participants were asked to name their favorite animal and to explain their choice. The question seemed a bit lame, but my seminarian confreres and I responded to it, although with varying degrees of seriousness. One selected the dolphin for its kindness and love of companionship. Another chose the fox for its cleverness while others also chose from the canine family— one the English setter for its intelligence and elegance, another the wolf for its intensity and concentration on the hunt!

In selecting my favorite animal I managed to overcome those nationalistic Australian sentiments that direct me toward the kangaroo, the koala, the wallaby, and the wombat. My favorite animal was and remains the majestic workhorse—the Belgian or the Clydesdale. This beautiful animal is at its best, at its most natural, noble, and full-hearted state when it is working as part of a team, whether this be pulling a plow for an Amish farmer in northern Indiana or the Budweiser beer wagon in a St. Patrick's Day parade.

I mention this not to prompt reflection on favorite animals and their meaning but rather because any reflection on work inevitably leads me to think of the simplicity and grace and natural quality of the draft horse in action. One senses in them a true and justified pride in their ability to get the job done. They display a recognition that work is not something to be shirked or avoided but rather how we best use our talents.

Work is sometimes an aspect of life about which we can have a real ambivalence. At college we can joke about avoiding it and evading it. Sometimes, in order to prevent ourselves being labeled "nerds" or "throats," we even disguise how much work we actually undertake, although this doesn't happen much before those big chemistry tests. Of course, work—whether it be intellectual or manual—requires an element of toil as we usually discover soon after graduation. It requires energy and effort and sweat from us. It can challenge us and extend us and reveal to us our limitations.

Whatever our ambivalence, however, it is good to remind ourselves of the importance of work and the central role it plays in our lives as Christians. Pope John Paul II in his encyclical *On Human Work* went so far as to suggest that through our work we can share in the very work of God's creation. What a noble enterprise and instructive way to conceive of the work we do and will do in the future!

Surely we all recognize the importance of work and its impact in shaping our lives. The editor of *Commonweal*, Margaret O'Brien Steinfels, expressed this well in her commencement address at Notre Dame:

Our work consumes us, and it also creates us. Much of the good—or evil—we do in this world will very likely be done through our work. That is why it is important to have work you love. Work you love will nourish and create you as you have been nourished and created in your families [and at college]. Above all, it will allow you to nourish others and create new possibilities, perhaps for people you will never know, whom you will never meet.

Your work is how most readily and directly you can bring Christ to the world and how you can serve and engage the world as a Christian. Your work and your vocation as a Christian man or woman should not be in separate compartments of your life. Your work, hopefully, is not simply a job.

In his fine book *Habits of the Heart*, the distinguished sociologist Robert Bellah outlined three stances which we can take toward work. The first is to see work as a job, as "a way of making money and earning a living." The second views work as a career, in which "work traces one's progress through life by achievement and advancement in an occupation." Lastly and in its strongest sense, Bellah suggests work can be understood as a calling in which it "constitutes a practical ideal of activity and character that makes a person's work morally inseparable from his or her life."

I don't want to dismiss the first two stances. You need to earn a living to support yourself and eventually your family, and also to pay off those inevitable college loans. Similarly, one needs to experience progression to different levels of responsibility in any occupation. But I want to insist that job and career are not enough if you are to see work as an important part of your Christian vocation. Here the sense of calling is crucial because it will reveal that your work has meaning for you beyond your paycheck and promotions. It will be the venue for you to join workmates in making real, as Bellah puts it, "the reign of God in the realm of work—that we all need each other, that we all depend on each other, and that our reward is our sense of contribution to the common good." Such an approach will directly influence *how* you undertake your work as teacher, doctor, engineer, businessperson, lawyer, public official, scholar, etc. It should influence how you select and determine what kinds of positions you will pursue and accept.

Seeing one's work as a way to live out a Christian vocation will influence not only what you do and how you do it but also how you relate to others who work. Folks with college education do far better in material terms in the high-tech/knowledge-based economy of the present than those men and women who went to work after graduation from high school or those who didn't achieve even that level of education. Gaps are widening in the earning power of these different groups. However that may be, don't see yourself as separate from or better than those who labor in what some might call more menial occupations. Treat with real respect and appreciation all those folk who labor honestly—the folk who serve us in the supermarket, clean our office buildings, cook our meals when we go out to eat.

Acknowledge and affirm folk in whatever calling they find themselves, however "lowly" it might seem. The need to work and to have that sense of making a contribution resides pretty deeply in everyone. I know this close-up from my own dad's experience. He was a hard-working man—a butcher—but he lost his sight following an accident at work. Naturally, dealing with his blindness presented many challenges for him, but among those he found most difficult was that he could no longer work to provide for his family. One day the publican at the local watering-hole where he occasionally would have a few beers with his brothers and mates offered him a part-time job helping in the pub's kitchen. This was "menial" work peeling the vegetables and so forth, but he could do it and he loved it. He was working again. I won't pretend that he saw his job as a "career" or a "calling," but I've always thought the publican better fulfilled his calling by allowing my dad to do this work.

When you assume positions of responsibility as you undoubtedly will as managers and owners of businesses, respect your workers' dignity. Take to heart Pope John Paul's instruction against seeing workers as simply "an instrument of production" on the same level as the material means of production. Accord the workers you supervise or employ the respect you expect to be shown to you.

With all this said about work, let me offer a cautionary note that work not come to dominate your life. With Americans locked into a seemingly irresistible desire for new or better consumer goods, lots of households go into debt to buy the products which advertisers suggest they need. To pay for them requires lots of work—work and spend, work and spend, and it never seems to stop. It's quite understandable why folk work so much given how they define their needs. Nevertheless, there are different kinds of need which deserve attention and are neglected if work totally dominates one's life. Here, I refer as you would expect to friendship, family life, direct service to others, participation in church, social, and civic groups, exercise, and leisure. Work is a part of your life. Work should not be your life.

I must confess that the sight of the team pulling the Budweiser wagon is a marvelous one for me. Above and beyond the beauty of the animals, however, I'm struck by their notable ability to work together. Their teamwork has an exhilarating quality, but it pales into insignificance when compared to the sight of Christian women and men engaged together in their vocations around the world. We have important tasks to perform and a job to do here in the Master's vineyard. Let us be about that work.

The Abortion Issue

"I have set before you life and death, the blessing and the curse. Choose life, then, that you and your descendants may live."

Abortion is a great moral issue and surely one of the most divisive political questions in this society. Whenever I speak about it, I do so with a little hesitation. One of the charges of the pro-abortion supporters is that the male, celibate clergy of the Catholic church—a group that is supposedly out of touch and unsympathetic to women—has prompted the opposition to abortion. This view got quite a run during this past decade because of the Vatican's efforts at the U.N. conferences in Cairo and Beijing. At these meetings the Vatican representatives tried to prevent the approval of abortion as a means of population control and to defend the integrity of women.

In reality, the efforts of priests and bishops in the pro-life movement have not been all that significant. I don't devote nearly enough time and effort in my preaching and ministry to this crucial issue, and many other priests are similarly guilty. We are not the motivators of this movement. The fact is that the pro-life movement which emerged in the early 1970s after *Roe v. Wade* legalized abortion has been a people's movement—a grassroots, bottom-up effort by literally thousands and thousands of ordinary folks.

What is usually neglected by the pro-abortion media is that the pro-life movement has from the outset been a women's movement. Women make up the majority of the volunteers who staff the help-centers for pregnant women. They make up the majority of members in the Right-to-Life chapters across the country. I don't think it is all that difficult to understand why this might be so. Women who have carried a baby to term know that the being who grows within them is not just some collection of cells. Instinctively and intuitively they rebel against the suggestion that any person has the right to destroy the developing baby.

We know, of course, that many others take a different point of view. Supporters of easy access to abortion never focus on what happens in an abortion. There is a vast denial here. Instead the supporters of abortion have changed the basic question from "Is abortion right or wrong?" to a rather different question: "Who decides?" They have argued most effectively that it is the woman who should decide. They have made a point of trying to prevent any others from being involved; hence their opposition to parental notification for teenagers or requirements that the father of the child be informed.

The "choice" strategy has been extremely effective. Lots of folks who have qualms about abortion are heard to say, "I'm personally opposed to abortion," or, "I would never have an abortion, but I don't want to impose my beliefs on others." No one wants to appear as "big brother." We all want to appear "tolerant" and "open." Thus there is a toleration of the "choice" to end the life of the developing baby.

Abortion is having a ripple effect throughout the society. It promotes a culture more tolerant of violence and death—a culture in which assisted suicide and so-called "mercy" killing are on the near horizon, and perhaps not far down the way are other horrendous practices that challenge the sanctity of life and the integrity and dignity of each human person. We confront a "culture of death," as Pope John Paul so well described in his encyclical *Evangelium Vitae* (*The Gospel of Life*).

The slavery analogy has been used often in the debate over abortion and it is telling. In 1857 the U.S. Supreme Court handed down the Dred Scott Decision. By a 7-2 vote it ruled that black slaves were not "legal persons," that they were the property of the slave owner. The abolitionists protested only to be met with this answer: "We understand you oppose slavery and that you find it morally offensive. That is your privilege. You don't have to own a slave if you don't want to. But don't impose your morality on the slave owner. He has the constitutionally protected right to choose to own a slave." In the famous Lincoln-Douglas debates, Stephen Douglas defended the right to choose. Abraham Lincoln's reply was: "No one has the right to choose to do what is so fundamentally wrong."

Can we hear Lincoln's voice today? We have laws that say parents cannot abuse a child and certainly, thank God, we have laws that prohibit infanticide, that say that a baby's life cannot be taken. We limit the "choice" of folks clearly and decisively in lots of areas when the societal consensus deems something to be wrong. Surely abortion should be in this category. In seeking this end, we fulfill an important dimension of Jesus' proclamation to stand with the weak ones in the society.

Know well, however, that if you "choose life" (Dt 30:19) and work for the pro-life cause, you will be on the unfashionable side of the issue as the mainstream media present it. Yet we have the Lord's ringing injunction to be not afraid to call us forth to action. We need it, for the challenge is substantial. Whatever the extent of the challenge, your generation is the one called to halt the societal moral decline of which abortion is such a disastrous manifestation. Among those reading these pages are men and women who can help build upon the heroic efforts of the present pro-life leaders.

Not all of us can be fighting the big public policy battles, but perhaps we might resolve to assist in meaningful ways women who are pregnant and decide to have their babies. Knowing the issues involved, let us resolve never to resort to abortion whatever the pressure applied. Let us "choose life." In the end let us reaffirm our deep gratitude for God's gift of life and resolve to allow all to share it.

> "Jesus said to them: 'I ask you, is it lawful to do good on the Sabbath—or evil? To preserve life—or destroy it?'"

Just Another Life

Bill Clinton is not my favorite American president. I had reservations about Clinton and his approach to politics from early on in his administration, long before the name Monica Lewinsky became a staple in the media. His contempt for the truth, his dumbing down of moral standards, his shameful veto of the bill outlawing the horrendous practice of partial-birth abortion all lay in the future when my reservations about the president first evolved. In fact I can identify the occasion when my uncertainty about Clinton developed into a more critical stance. This happened in 1993 when I read an article in the February 22 issue of *The New*

Yorker magazine by the writer Marshall Frady, the author of an excellent biography of the evangelist Billy Graham.

Marshall Frady provided a detailed and sad account of the January 1992 execution of a forty-year-old black convict named Rickey Ray Rector who had been condemned to death for killing a policeman in Conway, Arkansas, over ten years before. Rector's guilt was not contested. A deeply troubled person from childhood, his life had contained one brush with the law after another, culminating in his murder of a black man at a dance and soon afterward his cold-blooded killing of a white police officer, Robert Martin, in the parlor of the small home where Rector's mother lived.

Some might quickly conclude that this "cop-killer" got his just deserts and that justice was served with his execution. But the story, as Frady presented it, was more complicated. After killing Officer Martin, Rickey Ray Rector had gone out into his mother's backyard, lifted the pistol he held to his left temple, and pulled the trigger. As Frady reported, this "had left him with what amounted after surgery, to a frontal lobotomy and, according to subsequent testimony, with about the understanding of a young child—a dim simplicity that the surgeon who operated on him likened to that of the Jack Nicholson character after his lobotomy in *One Flew Over the Cuckoo's Nest*." Rector's mental impairment or retardation raised major questions about his competence to stand trial and to be executed, but the sentiment to avenge the murder of Officer Martin was deeply felt in Conway. Rector was tried, convicted, and sentenced to die. During one of his trials, his attorney posed the issue as: "The person who shot Officer Martin cannot be executed. He no longer lives. If we cannot execute that person, must we nevertheless execute his body?" The jury resoundingly answered yes.

By January 1992 Rector's various appeals had run their course. His sole hope relied on a clemency decision by then Arkansas Governor Bill Clinton. As the scheduled time of the execution approached, Governor Clinton was campaigning in New Hampshire for its upcoming primary; but his campaign had been rocked by tabloid allegations about his extramarital relationship with Gennifer Flowers. Despite the hemorrhaging of his political life brought on by the Flowers accusation, Clinton left New Hampshire and returned to Little Rock to be on hand to respond immediately to any final appeals and arguments on the execution day. Frady noted that "Clinton was not statutorily obliged to be in the state at all on the day of an execution." His lieutenant governor could exercise authority in his absence. But Clinton wanted to be back in Arkansas when the execution took place and the reasons for his decision sparked my reservations about him.

As Frady presented it, Clinton returned to Arkansas primarily for political reasons. This was an exercise in calculation and expediency because he wanted, as one of Rector's defense attorney's alleged, "to make the point that *he* did it." The Houston *Chronicle* later remarked: "Never—or at least not in the recent history of presidential campaigns—has a contender for the nation's highest elective office stepped off the campaign trail to ensure the killing of a prisoner." Clinton didn't waste much time on the day of Rector's execution attending to the matter. Plotting strategy to deal with the Flowers crisis came first. Only late in the day did he take a call from Rector's attorney, a lawyer who had grown up with Clinton in Hot Springs. He remained unmoved by the lawyer's plea that Rector was "a zombie, he doesn't understand death is permanent, he's a *child*. If you're gonna execute people, this is just not the appropriate one."

Rector's execution date had come at the wrong time. Friends close to Clinton believed that he would not have permitted the execution of Rector had he not been running for president. But this ferociously ambitious man planned to occupy the White House, and he would do what was needed to get there. He couldn't permit the perception that he was in any way soft either on crime or on criminals. He had seen what George Bush and the Republicans had done to Michael Dukakis four years earlier with the Willie

Horton matter. Here Clinton had an opportunity to draw some attention away from the Gennifer Flowers matter and, more important, to demonstrate his support for the death penalty by actually applying it. Rickey Ray Rector's life was in a certain sense a means to an end for him. Frady's rather chilling portrait of Clinton's politically-driven decision to allow the execution of Rector should not surprise us. Bill Clinton was simply a politician more skilled than most in seeking out the public mood and playing to it. Clinton was not a man motivated by some monstrous obsession to execute people. Of course not. He was motivated instead by his need to win elections—first in the Democratic primaries and then beyond. In seeking this end he knew well that the great majority of Americans, perhaps as high as eighty percent, favor the death penalty. He was not about to upset this constituency to preserve the life of Rickey Ray Rector.

One might have hoped for a greater display of political courage from Clinton or a more generous extension of mercy, but in the end Clinton simply catered to what the majority of citizens desired. He went along with the flow on this issue, and he certainly is not the only politician in America to do so. Since the mid-1970s men and women have increasingly pushed for the adoption of the death penalty. Now fewer than ten states refrain from consigning people to "death row." The death penalty proponents exploit easily the alleged sympathies of its opponents for brutal criminals over against the innocent victims. They understand well how an execution can ease the pain and bring a certain closure to a victim's relatives. They play effectively to deep impulses for revenge that lie within all of us. They exploit the fear and anger at the violence to which too many are subjected today.

Death penalty proponents don't seem disturbed that those executed tend to be men (and a few women) who, like Rector, have little education, low IQs, and have lived on the social and economic fringes of society. They don't seem perturbed that the victims of capital punishment tend often to have been provided with rather poor legal representation. They are only moderately shaken with the "mistakes" of the legal system which send innocent people to death row. The fact that since 1976 twenty states have released a total of seventy-six people previously sentenced to death gives them little pause. The possibility that innocent lives would be taken by state-sponsored execution is ignored. The chilling quality of the electric chair and of lethal injection fails to deter. Is it any wonder that pragmatic politicians like Clinton, unburdened with a set of principles and convictions to guide them, rush to demonstrate their credentials in support of the death penalty at election time?

Should young Catholic men and women be part of the constituency on this issue to which politicians so readily genuflect? I have no doubt that many are at this time. I certainly have heard the sentiment expressed vigorously that perpetrators of terrible crimes—like Timothy McVeigh or the Unabomber—should pay with their lives. They should "fry," as the expression goes.

Our church asks us, however, to take a more considered stance on this issue. Church teaching asks us to restrain the powerful emotions which lead us to demand a life for a life. The new *Catechism of the Catholic Church* sets forth this crucial principal: "If bloodless means are sufficient to defend human lives against an aggressor and to protect public order and the safety of persons, public authority must limit itself to such means, because they better correspond to the concrete conditions of the common good and are more in conformity to the dignity of the human person" (#2267). Executions fall well outside the parameters of these "bloodless means."

This teaching is not easy to "sell" in a political context. It commends to us that we take appropriate measures to punish the perpetrator of crimes and to defend the common good of the society by removing the danger of this perpetrator causing any further harm. But it asks that even the life of brutal criminals be treated with some mercy. It asks that no further blood be spilled. It calls us to move beyond the motives of revenge and to see instead the damage done to the society when our hearts are so hardened as to demand this irreversible form of punishment. Church teaching says to us that respect for life throughout the society will be strengthened when even terribly flawed and savage lives are accorded some respect and not treated as so beyond redemption that they must be destroyed. Refusing to take these lives raises the societal sense of the preciousness of all life and aligns us with Jesus' call to "preserve life" (Lk 6:9).

Let us not pretend that this is an easy teaching. It is not. It is, however, important if we are ever to stem the erosion of respect for life which is so manifest in the abortion holocaust and in the developing support for assisted suicide, mercy killing, and euthanasia. Young Catholics who value life and want to defend it will not succumb to powerful appeals of the death penalty proponents. Young Catholics who reflect in their lives the gospel of life and Christ's sustaining message of healing love won't turn their backs on those condemned to die. They will refrain from participating in any way in the culture of death.

Even more so, pro-life Catholics will work to restrain the use of the death penalty. Here one must issue a special call to the Catholic lawyers of the future. You will be the ones who serve in the judicial system. Let your service include offering adequate defense to those likely to be sentenced to die. Doing so may not help any future presidential campaign you launch, but it may help save a life. That in the end will be worth your doing.

"Always seek
one another's
good, and for
that matter,
the good
of all."

Needed: Catholic Politicians

Catholics participated in American public life right from the outset. The eloquent Charles Carroll of Carrollton, Maryland, signed the Declaration of Independence and leads off a long list of Catholics who have participated vigorously in American politics. In the late nineteenth century as European immigrants poured into the cities of the Northeast and Midwest, Catholics—especially Irish-Catholics—gravitated to political activity, established political machines, and came to dominate the governments of cities like New York, Boston, Philadelphia, and Chicago. They came in the twentieth century to form a key component of the Democratic Party, albeit one that rested uneasily with another key element of that party's amazing coalition—the white Protestant South.

Despite this influence and participation there remained an ambivalence about Catholic involvement in American politics. Catholics were held to be suspect in their commitment to the United States. Where, it was asked, did their loyalties ultimately lie—with their church or with their nation? This issue received a full airing during New York Governor Al Smith's failed bid for the presidency in 1928. Some voters clearly held Smith's religion against him, and the conclusion was drawn that a Catholic could not be elected to the nation's highest office. Catholicism constituted some sort of risk to the American experiment.

John F. Kennedy's election to the presidency in 1960 seemed to shatter the political barrier obstructing America's acceptance of Catholicism. The concurrent election of one hundred Catholics to the Congress (eighty-nine to the House and eleven to the Senate) appeared to confirm the point. The 1960 election increased Catholic optimism and reduced the psychological defensiveness which had been evident right through the 1950s. Kennedy's idealism, his apparent willingness to conquer new frontiers, and then his tragic assassination locked him into a revered position in the American public mind where he remains well-lodged. Certainly Catholics accorded him reverential treatment. Andrew Greeley even asked seriously in 1967 if John Kennedy should not be canonized because he had "put to rest forever the fear that Catholicism was an alien religion and that Catholic political leaders would use their positions to interfere with American freedoms."

Yet, in the perspective provided by the passage of the subsequent decades, it now is clear that the election of a Catholic to the presidency meant little in terms of the tangible impact of Catholics on public policy. This conclusion may be a painful one for those many Catholics for whom JFK's thousand days in office still exert a mythic attraction. But it is one which must be accepted if an understanding of Catholic influence on public policy is to be obtained.

Sadly, the election of John Kennedy meant only a conditional acceptance of Catholicism into the mainstream of American life. It was an acceptance made on conditions which Kennedy explicitly promised to accept, most notably in his meeting with the Protestant ministers in Houston, that he would consign his religion to a purely private status and that he would not act on public policy in any recognizably Catholic way. JFK found it easier to make this promise, it seems, because his religion was of no special importance to him as a guide for life. Both his critics like Garry Wills, who finds Kennedy "rootless," and sympathetic court historians like Arthur Schlesinger Jr., who claims that "he took religion . . . with detachment" and describes Kennedy's ethos as "more [classical] Greek than Catholic," agree on this.

Forgive this little discourse on John Kennedy. I wish it were simply of some limited historical interest. Regrettably it is much more, because Kennedy proved a central figure in influencing the behavior of many subsequent politicians who were Catholics. They too chose to follow the JFK pattern and to consign their religion to the private sphere. This has been most dramatically seen in the legion of politicians who list themselves as Catholics and claim to be "personally opposed" to abortion but who refuse to act on that conviction in the domain of public policy. In their decisions rests a significant reason for the sizable dearth of genuine conviction, principle, and moral discourse in American political life. These politicians separate moral convictions from political actions.

Some politicians have tried to defend this course. Most notably in a well-known address at Notre Dame in 1984, then New York Governor Mario Cuomo announced he accepted the teaching authority of his church and its position on abortion. But he refused to concede that this should lead him to support either legislation or a constitutional amendment to limit or ban abortion. Instead, he appealed to "Catholic realism," suggesting that any ban on abortion would be divisive and would not work anyway. Thus his fundamental principle: "The values derived from religious belief will not—should not—be accepted as part of the public morality unless they are shared by the pluralistic community at large, by consensus."

Thoughtful observers relentlessly dismantled Cuomo's "Catholic realism" principle, asking if it should have been applied to other great moral questions such as racial discrimination. And Cuomo's refusal to do anything to build further a consensus in opposition to abortion confirmed the essential bankruptcy of his stance. If he had insisted that abortion was morally wrong, an evil which needed first to be contained and then placed "in the course of ultimate extinction" (as Lincoln said of slavery in 1858), his position might have proved more defensible. A case for genuine Catholic realism might have been made on this foundation. Instead he insisted on campaigning to make abortion more readily available. He defended the most permissive abortion regime of any democratic nation, even when it was obvious that the American public consensus did not favor abortion on demand and in fact preferred restraints on access to abortion.

It is hard to identify a distinctive Catholic contribution to American political life in the eighties and nineties. With notable exceptions like Robert P. Casey, the determined pro-life advocate and former governor of Pennsylvania, Catholic politicians tended to blend in and refrained from utilizing their religion as an inspiration and guide for their actions. And this despite the fact that the fundamental problems of the American polity and society—the decline of family and community, unrestrained individualism at the expense of the common good, rampant relativism in values—presented a unique opportunity and challenge to Catholics in the political domain. The theologian Richard John Neuhaus—with good reason—termed this circumstance "the Catholic moment," but it passed without an effective Catholic response. Three decades after the Second Vatican Council challenged Catholics to be "leaven in the world," they are well on their way to being unrecognizable in the political domain.

Will your generation placidly accept this situation as just "the way things are"? Or are there women and men among your number who refuse to be deterred by the pervasive cynicism in which politicians and political institutions are held today? Are there potential political leaders among you who appreciate that religious and moral convictions are not private possessions and do not depend upon the existence of a "consensus" in order to be exercised, who understand well that opinion polls do not determine what is right and true? Are there young Catholics who understand that their church's teachings—on respect for human life, on concern for the common good, on responsibilities as well as individual rights, on the utility of the principle of subsidiarity (which holds that decisions should be made as close as possible to the local level), and on the importance of family and community—have something important to contribute to American politics? Are there young Catholics who can translate these broad teachings into sound policies and programs for "the good of all" (1 Thes 5:15) and help Americans live better together?

My observations of and conversations with students tells me that there is a reservoir of goodness and commitment in your generation that can bring about a true regeneration of Catholic commitment to American political life. Among your generation are talented women and men who won't always place their own interests first and who will speak truthfully and act with integrity. If you feel some call to serve in this way, respond to it. Politics is an honorable profession which desperately needs women and men who act from motives deeper than poll-driven calculations of personal advantage. Such politicians are needed at all levels and in both of the great political parties.

In his inaugural address on that cold and bright January day in 1961, John F. Kennedy told his fellow Americans: "Ask not what your country can do for you; ask what you can do for your country." His eloquent words still stir a response, and rightly so. Today, however, the country needs people who don't simply have a disposition to serve but who know how to serve well and rightly. Let us pray that there are those among us who will rest their service firmly on a moral base, unafraid to serve both their nation and their God.

> "One who is a teacher should use that gift for teaching."

Go Teach

"**W**hy not be a teacher?" asks Sir Thomas More of the ambitious young Richard Rich in an oft-quoted passage from Robert Bolt's play *A Man for All Seasons*. More assures Rich that "You'd be a fine teacher. Perhaps a great one." Not persuaded, Rich replies, "And if I was, who would know it?" More tells him plainly, "You, your pupils, your friends, God. Not a bad public that. And, oh, a quiet life." Well, More's final comment regarding a quiet life is perhaps a little suspect given the diverse challenges of teaching today, but his insight about audience is still largely accurate. Teaching does not attract great public attention or the material rewards of some other professions. It remains, however, among the most crucial professions and callings.

Teachers, along with parents, bear the main responsibility for the education of the young. They are key in passing on the wisdom of one generation to another. Teaching is among the most important of human activities. The teacher must know this in her or his heart. Good teachers understand deeply that they are engaged in an important and a sacred calling. They call others forth to develop their talents and character.

The need is great for good and talented folk to enter the ranks of the teaching profession. That certainly goes for teachers at all levels and in all subjects and in both the public and private systems. I want, however, to give a special call to young Catholic college students and recent graduates to consider working in the Catholic school system in its many and various dimensions. Catholic education seen broadly has done more to liberate people, more to lift folk from poverty than any other ministry in which the church is involved. It is also a crucial vehicle for evangelization and religious formation. Some critics over the past few decades have presented education as a traditional and institutional apostolic activity. Some members of religious orders have retreated from it in search of more "cutting-edge" ministries. They were mistaken. The reality is that education remains among the most dynamic and important ministries in the church.

The success of Catholic schools measured in academic criteria is now a subject of regular commentary in the social science literature. Catholic schools are far more successful than public schools, and especially with minority students. In explaining this Abigail Thernstrom has noted the importance of "the sense of school unity" evident in them and further explicated:

> The principal hires the staff and chooses people who endorse the school's ideals. Those in authority thus speak with one voice. They share both an educational outlook and extraordinary commitments to the students. Teaching is not a job, they say; it is a calling. Teachers have a mission: to do good. That

outlook creates a special atmosphere. The teachers get to know every student. The school becomes family.

In the end, the ethos of the school counts most.

Sadly, the generations of sisters, brothers, and priests who staffed the Catholic schools and helped give them such a distinctive ethos are aging and passing from the scene. New men and women capable of continuing their work are needed. Some, hopefully, will be brothers, sisters, and priests, but the vast majority will be committed lay-women and laymen. Such men and women will play their part in making the church truly and effectively present in the world by creating school communities in which, as the British writer Vincent Nichols notes, "everyone tries to live out their faith, expressing it in daily living, celebrating it in prayer and liturgy, and sharing it with others by word and example."

George Bernard Shaw's remark that "those who can, do; those who can't, teach" is occasionally thrown out as a criticism of teachers. This bears the implication that any-body could be a teacher. This is a quite widespread view on university campuses. It is one that doesn't bear even lim-ited analysis. Anyone who has sat through a lousy class taught by a knowledgeable professor can testify to that. Having knowledge in your head is not sufficient to be a teacher. A teacher must be able to convey that knowledge. It's not an easy undertaking, and you should not think it so. Teaching is a difficult and an individual art. I speak of it as an art because it's not just a skill that you can learn. It's much more than that. The art of an individual teacher is as illusive as the art of a painter or a sculptor.

There's only one general criterion that I would set forth for a teacher: he or she should enjoy teaching. This doesn't mean that you'll enjoy it every single day, every single moment. But at a sort of gut level you must know that this is the calling that provides you with such satisfaction that you know it is what you were meant to do.

Every good teacher is engaged in developing talents and minds. Teachers in Catholic schools are explicitly aiming to do more. They seek also to be involved in forming character and shaping souls. In a Catholic school you are called to teach the virtues and not to pretend that moral education is outside your domain. You are to engage the boys and girls, the young men and the young women you will teach as whole people, to engage the whole person. This aspect of teaching has in some ways been lost in college and university teaching. Many faculty members, sadly, are reluctant to engage in this approach. It should be reclaimed in our colleges and universities and certainly continued in Catholic schools.

Regardless of the particular subject that you will teach, you should be concerned with the conduct of life in all your teaching. Beyond the knowledge transmitted and the thinking skills that are nurtured in students is the centrality of values, of questions regarding how to live. If you want to live your vocation as a teacher by seeking to train minds, to form characters, to shape souls, it will be best done by more than direct instruction. The forming of character and the shaping of souls is done more by witness. Pope Paul VI made a perceptive remark that "modern man listens more willingly to witnesses than to teachers, and if he does listen to teachers, it is because they are witnesses." You will find that it's difficult for any teacher to avoid being treated to some extent as a model or exemplar. You may not always seek out this responsibility, but you won't be able to avoid it. A good teacher can convey the value of honesty, perseverance, self-discipline, moral courage, and commitment to truth very well by how she or he goes about teaching. A poor teacher, of course, fosters indifference and stifles or deadens whatever curiosity and enthusiasm students bring to their studies.

All Christian teachers have a distinct call. They are called to be witnesses to the gospel in their lives. Fr. Nicholas Ayo, C.S.C., says teachers should "give witness to our grasp of truth and love of goodness. We cry the gospel with our lives." He suggests that students will learn what full humanity might entail and what is the awesome range of gifts and talents they could explore from the reading of living books—teachers. If one is to be a true witness to the gospel, then one's disposition must surely be one of service. The teacher must really be servant to the students. You have certain talents and skills and training—a "gift for teaching" in the words of St. Paul (Rom 12:7)—which you can apply for the benefit of others. Neither man nor woman lives by bread alone. You can enrich and nourish minds and hearts and souls.

It's interesting to recall that the most common title used by people in addressing Jesus was "Rabbi" or "teacher." That was surely a predominant aspect of his ministry. His classroom was the mountainside or the lakeshore or the private home, wherever he found people. The context of your ministry most likely will be a school, but it is a location in which you can fully live out your discipleship of Jesus Christ.

Whether or not you seek to follow Jesus as a Catholic teacher, I pray each of you will recognize the importance of Catholic education. Catholic schools at all levels are key locales for education in the faith. Education and evangelization are interwoven in their missions. One scholar has argued that teaching has been the most universal and most appreciated aspect of Christian ministry throughout the ages. Your generation must ensure this remains so long into this new millennium.

Priest
(_&_ Teacher)

"Go into the whole world and proclaim the good news to all creation."

Priesthood in the church is the vocation to which God called me. It is as priest that I seek to live out the common call to discipleship shared by all believers. Through the mystery of the priesthood and the sacrament of ordination I have been claimed permanently for service in the church. The call and claim of priesthood have come to me as a gift from God, and it is one for which I am profoundly grateful.

Priestly ministry occasionally appears to be in flux today, but I have not really found it so. The priest's vocation still calls him to preside at eucharist. It still calls him to proclaim the word of God and to preach about it with authenticity. It still calls him to speak words of forgiveness, consolation, compassion, and encouragement. It still calls him to share the life of Christ with others. This is what good priests have done for centuries and what they must continue to do.

The priestly life is a good life. It is not always easy—at least I have not always found it so—but what of value is? Yet this life brings joys and blessings in good measure. One has the pleasure of being invited into homes and the fun of sharing the family meal with many different families. One is granted the privilege of being allowed to assist people in their time of need. One has a marvelous vantage point to observe grace powerfully at work in peoples' lives—the sheer wonder of witnessing broken spirits being mended and defeated folk finding new strength. There is a deep sense in my priestly life of being carried along in my weakness by those among whom I minister and of being blessed by those whom I bless.

If you hear a call to this life—and it usually starts as some vague feeling deep in your gut—don't run from it or try to dismiss it. Listen well to it and respond. This may indeed be what the Lord is calling you by name to do. You might have hesitations and doubts, but rest assured that God somehow taps one's courage and generosity in ways you might not have thought yourself capable. God's grace will sustain you. And if you know someone who senses this call, extend your support to them. This may be a part of how you play your role in building up the church.

My own journey to and in the priesthood involved me in some significant separation from my family and my country. I sensed, however, that the Lord called me to the Congregation of Holy Cross—the order I had come to know when I was a student at Notre Dame. I knew deeply that within this community and perhaps within its ministry of higher education, I might seek to "proclaim the good news" (Mk 16:15), to talk with others about Christ, and to join them in walking his way. Subsequently, I have grown to appreciate well that I exercise my ministry as a priest as part of the larger apostolic effort of my religious order, which I find a blessing.

In the Congregation of Holy Cross I utilize my training as a historian, and whatever my gifts for teaching, as part of my calling as a priest. I am a priest who also teaches—a priest-teacher. I preach the word of God, preside at liturgy, strive to build up the community, and I teach. I don't have a bifurcated calling in which I switch hats from "teacher" at one moment to "priest" at another. I am a priest. My teaching and scholarship are subsumed within that basic calling. Let me tell you just a little of how I have lived this calling as a priest-teacher and how I try to live it now.

I was ordained a priest on April 9, 1988, and was assigned (in the words of my religious superior's letter of obedience) "to reside and assist at the University of Notre Dame." I began my teaching with a strong sense that I was engaged upon a spiritual undertaking, that teaching was an important part of my priestly ministry. I knew that I was about not only improving minds but also shaping souls, that I was called to nurture not only the intellectual lives of my students but also their religious and moral lives and, indeed, to aid them in integrating the two.

I recognized that a crucial responsibility of the priest is to be a minister of the Word and appreciated well that preaching the Word could not be limited to the pulpit. It needed to be accomplished outside of the sanctuary, and by teachers beyond the discipline of theology. I thought, and still think, that the call of the priest who teaches must involve in some way bringing people to hear the word of God. Now, this might be done by relating the gospel to the issues raised in courses. I try to do this in some limited ways in my courses on American political and diplomatic history. I also have adopted some other approaches.

I decided from the outset, prompted by the witness of my own marvelous teachers, Fr. Thomas Blantz, C.S.C., and Fr. Robert Kerby, that I should pray to begin class. Leading my classroom "community" in prayer has been, in ways that are not easily explained, an important part of my ministry. Let me quickly make clear that the brief prayers of petition and thanksgiving offered by me or my students are hardly among the more eloquent ones aimed at heaven. I don't think I've managed to transform any class of mine into a prayer in the manner that Simone Weil suggests in her essay "Reflections on the Right Use of School Studies with a View to the Love of God." I wish I had. Instead, I've simply joined my students in praising God and in praying for a variety of matters, many of which simply develop from the rhythms of student life—to use gifts and talents generously, for wisdom and guidance in making decisions, to act as true friends, and so on. I believe that this brief prayer helps develop community in the classroom, and in small but perceptible ways the faith of each one who prays is affirmed and nourished.

As well as praying with students, I set out to join them as a guide (if that is not too exalted a term) on the journey of life. Perhaps I should modify my pretentious claim and say more simply that I aim to be available as a friend and informal counselor. I try to make known my concern for the whole person. I try, most basically, to get to know my students not as those individuals who attend my lectures and write papers and exams, but as people in the full sense—as men and women with not only minds but hearts and souls as well.

In this context I try to awaken and deepen each individual's sense of his or her own capacities and giftedness and to challenge all to use their gifts well and in the service of others. I try to stress that most of us are not called to withdraw from the world but to live as Christians in the midst of it, to be active in the world and engage it, to be "leaven." I place an emphasis on engaging in public life and service. Perhaps I apply in an offhand and preemptory way some of Woodrow Wilson's themes from his famous address "Princeton in the Nation's Service," in which he described his college as serving the nation by training its leaders to be people of character and possessing the ideal of service. But I hope it isn't mere repetition of Wilson. I trust my students hear from me that they are not simply to serve the nation on any terms; they are to be, with Saint

Thomas More, "the King's good servant, but God's first," with all that implies.

Along with my efforts to witness and to serve, to pray with and call forth the talents of my students, I engage in more public priestly "work." And, in fact, my teaching leads to other dimensions: students coming for reconciliation; my presiding at eucharist for different groups of students; and also, as the years pass, my presiding at the marriage celebrations of former students and my baptizing their babies. My teaching has not taken me *away* from priesthood but has been integral *to* it.

My years since ordination have been a graced time. Except when I'm grading lots of papers or exams and complaining about it, my teaching has been a joy. I make no great effort to disguise it. I like my students and, as we travel a bit together, hopefully some genuine learning takes place. I hope to go on doing what I'm doing for a long time. It's pretty straightforward and uncomplicated, but I sense deeply the Lord's presence in the work.

On this journey, which has taken me far from my own country, I am fortunate to have good companions—faith-filled collaborators in the Congregation of Holy Cross. I learn from their words and witness and benefit from their encouragement and support. I try to reciprocate as a brother should. Together we are engaged in a crucial ministry of the church.

Perhaps some of you who read this reflection might feel some call to this ministry of Catholic higher education. If so, I hope you will join us and be about the work God has provided. Others may sense a call to a different type of priestly ministry. I pray you will act on that call.

We live in an interesting and challenging time in the church. The path ahead is not necessarily an easy one. Yet we are called forward by the Lord's ringing counsel to "Be not afraid!" Don't let fear hold you back from this distinct call from God. The church—God's holy people—needs you.

Pope & Parish

"The community of believers were of one heart and one mind."

Catholics hold that the bishop of Rome is the successor to Saint Peter, the rock upon whom the Lord designated that the church be built (Mt 16:13-20). The papacy is an office of central importance in the Catholic tradition. The papacy has always distinguished Catholics from other Christians, and it still does. Catholics cannot see themselves as members of independent communities beholden only to themselves. Far from being islands unto ourselves we are linked directly to and joined with faith communities throughout the world. The successor of Peter serves as a focal point of unity for us. The papacy serves each of us by being a source of this unity.

The evangelizing missions and extensive travels of Pope John Paul II have highlighted this key function of the papal office in the church. He has journeyed to all parts of the world proclaiming the good news and calling Christians forth to transform their cultures. I remember once viewing some magnificent photographs taken during Pope John Paul's visit to Mt. Hagen, which is deep in the highlands of Papua New Guinea. Here the pope was greeted by ten thousand tribesmen and women wearing their traditional costumes. There was quite a contrast between the pope's traditional white soutane and the much more colorful garb of the locals which covered much less of their bodies. The joy-filled highlanders were carrying spears and dancing and singing. It was a marvelous scene. Though these folks had first heard the word of God within the last two generations, they connected readily through John Paul II to the larger church. His presence with them bonded them to the church universal. We should be grateful to the pope for this service of unifying us and linking us together, and we should not forget to pray for him in his special ministry.

Pope John Paul II now is an old man and, as you would know from seeing him on television, he is not the vigorous man elected to the papacy in 1978. In over two decades as pope he has played, at least in North America, to what the theater people might call "mixed reviews." Secular commentators and some more liberal Catholic theologians have deemed him out of step with his times, as conservative and overly concerned to enforce orthodoxy especially in matters of sexual ethics. Such criticisms seem rather puny and misdirected when the full range of concerns of his pontificate are considered. These criticisms emerge out of a liberal-conservative approach to church "politics" that seems rather tiresome and outdated. John Paul II certainly has transcended these categories.

When Karol Jozef Wojtyla is called home to meet his maker—and let us hope he lives long beyond the Great Jubilee he so much wants to experience—he will have left an indelible mark on the history of his time. He played a crucial role in bringing about the collapse of communism in Eastern Europe. Under his leadership the Catholic church emerged as a crucial defender of basic human rights throughout the world. He has issued a series of powerful and distinctive social encyclicals which built on past Catholic teaching to offer a profound and convincing critique of contemporary social and political orders and structures.

Beyond his contributions in the social and political realms, however, John Paul II has called upon the church to engage in the "new evangelization." The pope eagerly fostered the gospel's encounter with the culture of our time. For him the gospel must be proclaimed and the struggle for the world's soul pursued with true passion. John Paul has been a teacher and a guide for each of us to engage in this work of evangelization. He always has seen that young men and women have a special call in this regard.

Surprisingly, many Catholic students, including those who openly admire the pope, move through their years of college study without ever encountering the teaching instruction which John Paul II has given to guide us in our evangelizing mission. Sadly, this can even be the case for those who study in Catholic colleges and universities and who take a number of theology courses. Not to worry, you have it easily within your power to rectify that situation. I commend to you the pope's book *Crossing the Threshold of Hope*, in which he speaks clearly and accessibly about the existence of God and the dignity of persons, about pain, suffering, and evil, about eternal life and salvation, about hope and much else. His message is the Lord's: "Be not afraid."

Once you have completed that, I commend to you *Veritatis Splendor* (*The Splendor of Truth*), the pope's encyclical letter of August 6, 1993. Now you might not be in the habit of reading encyclical letters. I know I have skipped a few over the years. But this formidable document will more than repay your effort to read it. It asks fundamental questions: "What must I do? How do I distinguish good from evil?" The pope explores how the church "offers to everyone the answer which comes from the truth about Jesus Christ and his Gospel."

In addition to engaging the thought of Pope John Paul carefully, young Catholics today have a special obligation to *be* church. You are called to be the bearers of the new evangelization in the world. You are called to transform and claim the world for Christ. This is done for the most part in our work in the world, but our local parish should be a special place for us to be nourished in our efforts and to support each other in our Christian vocations. The parish, where we come together at eucharist to praise and worship God, should be a key base from which we set out on our mission.

I keep in touch with a good number of recent college graduates—and not only from my own school. A surprising number report some difficulty in moving to a new setting. Can you believe it—they miss college! Of course, some probing reveals that they don't really miss their professors (well, not that much) or their studies (some are engaged in more advanced graduate work). They miss on a deep level the friends and bonds of friendship made during their college years. Friends are now scattered all over the country, and despite phone and e-mail, it gets harder to keep in touch. Everyone is working or in graduate school, and somehow there don't seem to be too many welcoming communities around.

A good number of folk also miss the liturgies that they attended with their friends in their campus chapels or Newman Centers. These seem to have had a warmth and a relevance which they miss. Some complain to me about the parishes they attend or, in some cases, decline to attend. These parishes are reportedly "dull," or too focused on families with kids. My recently graduated friends sense they are on the periphery. Some use this as an excuse to salve their consciences as they remove going to Mass from their weekly commitments. Folks give up and disengage from the church.

This disengagement seems to be especially prevalent for young men. Single men are certainly the least likely to attend church in this society. Long free of parental influence and with the appeal of campus liturgies gone, many drop out of faithful practice and resume again only when marriage and children call them to terms with what they truly value in life. Sadly, some never really return. They drift away.

In the face of this reality I encourage young Catholic graduates to see involvement in a new parish as just as important and even more so than their settling in to their new job in the town or city to which they have moved. Register at your parish for a start. Don't be a nomad traveling around searching for the perfect liturgy to replicate your college experience. Get to know people within the parish community and join them in witnessing to the risen Lord. Put your gifts and talents at the disposal of the parish. Contemporary parishes cry out for young people—the twenty-somethings—to bring their gifts and talents to bear. Don't see yourself simply as a consumer in your parish asking what you get out of it. The writer Kathleen Norris has it right when she says, "the church is to be participated in and not consumed." Yours is the age group that can best work with teenagers and can help immeasurably in the training of the young. You are needed to work with the youth group, to teach CCD, and to help out at the local parochial school. You have the energy and commitment to others to work the lines in soup kitchens, to tutor in adult literacy programs, to tend to patients in hospices.

I must extend a special challenge and call to my male readers. In the United States today women heavily outnumber men in their participation in most church activities. According to the Notre Dame Study of Catholic Parish Life, more their eighty-five percent of those involved in ministry to the poor, sick, grieving, and handicapped are women. More than eighty percent of CCD teachers and sponsors of the catechumenate are women. Sixty percent of those involved in youth ministries are women. Men too must play their part. Strong and good men do this. As a bonus, I might add, church can be a wonderful place to meet new people, and to get to know them better than in chance encounters at bars, crowded parties, or the health club!

From Mt. Hagen in Papua New Guinea to whichever parish we find ourselves, John Paul II issues the same call to Catholics to live and proclaim the gospel. In this mission, believers should be "of one heart and one mind" (Acts 4:32). Ultimately faith is best proclaimed in and through the life of a believing community, and for most of us this means our parish. Dear parishioners (both present and future), don't be passive bystanders. Bring your spirit and energy to bear so that your parish may better participate in our crucial mission of evangelization.

Keep
the Faith

"You, then, are the body of Christ."

[The class of 1992 at the University of Notre Dame elected me the senior class fellow. During the week of graduation activities I gave a short address in Sacred Heart Basilica and offered some words of thanks and farewell. That now seems a long time ago. I'm older (and perhaps even wiser!) now, but I offer a slightly modified section of my talk in hope that it brings together into a fitting conclusion the points I have tried to make in this book.]

I want to talk about faith, and to help guide my thoughts I borrow from three "texts." The first is a modification of an Australian beer advertisement. The second is some counsel from my Mum. The last is a horrendous greeting card-type platitude.

Faith is best lived and proclaimed in community as you have demonstrated during your time here. As you leave, I pray that you will assume the role of community builders. Be folk who call forth the gifts of others, who reconcile differences, and who inject vitality and life into the communities you will join. When I was growing up, there was a line from an advertising jingle for my now favorite beer, Fourex—some of which I consume (in moderation of course) whenever I visit down under. The line went like this: "You need a big, big beer for a big, big thirst"—and, of course, Fourex was that beer. This line got picked up on and varied in certain ways. An old nun who taught me used to say, "I've got a big, big stick for a bad, bad boy"— and predictably, she threatened to use it a lot! But, no surprise, I have my own variation: "We have a big, big God for a big, big church," and there is room within it for us all. Whatever our interests and talents, we need to do our part to be the church, to help shape it—to enflesh "the body of Christ" (1 Cor 13:27).

One day, when I was a boy, I was rambling on to my Mum, who was doing some ironing at the time, as I recall. I was sharing with her my ambitions to play rugby for Australia and to serve as Prime Minister of the country, perhaps simultaneously! She cut me short by refusing to endorse my ambitions. She said simply, "All I want you to be is a good boy," and she said it in a tone that conveyed that this was more than an effort to get me to behave there and then. The old girl was on to something and she has worked the theme ever since, although sometimes a little tiresomely.

We live in a culture and society that focuses much on achievement and accomplishment. It infects everyone, it seems. I hope, however, that as you venture forth from this place you have a profound sense of yourself as a daughter or son of God—each of you precious in God's sight and each of you called personally to live a life inspired by the gospel rather than simply conforming to the dictates of our time. I pray you will live a life, in short, that is *good*; a life in which your faith will not be sequestered into some private domain but will guide all your commitments and actions. Be aware that this may mean that you won't be "in" with a certain crowd. But persevere in what you believe to be right and true.

Some time ago I was over at Holy Cross House (my order's retirement home). On the notice board there I saw a little poster which read, "You need both rain and sunshine to have a rainbow!" Frankly, I didn't know whether to laugh or to barf, but in the end I chuckled in a superior sort of way and thought: "O, God, I hope they don't subject me to this fuzzy stuff when I'm over here." But, embarrassing as it may be to admit it, those darn words stuck in my head. In the end, I took them as a sign that the Lord thought I should make an ass of myself and use them. Let me do so now. We know from our own experience that life is not all sunshine. I suspect that your years as a student have probably made that clear in various ways. But, hopefully, your experience has deepened your capacity to persevere in faith whatever rain may fall. Such perseverance in faith brings joy.

My friends, our religion, our faith, does not take us out of life but energizes and gives meaning to everyday life. It links us in solidarity to a community that stretches back 2,000 years. This community has gone through history, ever changing and adapting, in one century never the same as before, its doors always open to the world. It has been sustained by men and women such as yourselves—the merciful, the single-hearted, the peacemakers. In all that time the hungry have been fed, the sick have been comforted, the strangers have been welcomed and prisoners visited. And, deep in their hearts, men and women have discovered what makes life truly worthwhile. Dear readers of this book, keep the faith! Keep the faith, and in so doing, live it and share it.

Appendix

A Few Things a Catholic Should Know

The Ten Commandments

1. I am the Lord your God: you shall not have strange Gods before me.
2. You shall not take the name of the Lord your God in vain.
3. Keep holy the Sabbath day.
4. Honor your father and mother.
5. You shall not kill.
6. You shall not commit adultery.
7. You shall not steal.
8. You shall not bear false witness.
9. You shall not covet your neighbor's wife.
10. You shall not covet your neighbor's goods.

The Seven Sacraments

1. Baptism
2. Confirmation
3. Eucharist
4. Penance
5. Anointing of the sick or dying
6. Holy Orders
7. Matrimony

The Gifts of the Holy Spirit

1. Wisdom
2. Understanding
3. Counsel
4. Fortitude
5. Knowledge
6. Piety
7. Fear of the Lord

The Eight Beatitudes

1. Blessed are the poor in spirit.
2. Blessed are they that mourn.
3. Blessed are the meek.
4. Blessed are they that seek justice.
5. Blessed are the merciful.
6. Blessed are the chaste.
7. Blessed are the peacemakers.
8. Blessed are they that suffer persecution for the sake of justice.

The Seven Capital Sins or Vices and Their Opposite Virtues

1. Pride (Humility)
2. Greed (Generosity)
3. Lust (Chastity)
4. Unjustifiable Anger (Meekness)
5. Gluttony (Temperance)
6. Envy (Brotherly Love)
7. Sloth (Diligence)

The Theological Virtues

1. Faith
2. Hope
3. Charity

The Cardinal Virtues

1. Prudence
2. Justice
3. Fortitude
4. Temperance

The Two Great Commandments of Christ

1. You shall love the Lord your God with your whole heart, and with your whole soul, and with your whole mind, and with your whole strength.
2. You shall love your neighbor as yourself.

The Corporal Works of Mercy

1. To feed the hungry
2. To give drink to the thirsty
3. To clothe the naked
4. To comfort the sorrowful
5. To bear wrongs patiently
6. To forgive injuries
7. To pray for the living and dead

The Three Great Good Works

1. Prayer
2. Fasting
3. Giving alms to the needy

The Evangelical Counsels

1. Poverty
2. Chastity
3. Obedience

The Golden Rule

Do unto others as you want them to do to you.

A Note on Sources

These reflections rely on a wide range of reading and discussion over recent years. Scripture, especially the gospels, provide the starting point for some of them. I also draw on the *Catechism of the Catholic Church* (Washington, D.C.: U.S. Catholic Conference, 1994) and some of the encyclicals of Pope John Paul II. Among the latter one might pay special attention to his *Laborem Exercens* (On Human Work), September 14, 1981; *Veritatis Splendor* (The Splendor of the Truth), August 6, 1993; and *Evangelium Vitae* (The Gospel of Life), March 25, 1995. An easy introduction to the pope's thinking comes in his *Crossing the Threshold of Hope* (New York: Alfred A. Knopf, 1995). Also note his *Letter to Women* (June 1995) which testifies movingly to the "genius of women." Important documents from the Second Vatican Council, including *Gaudium et Spes*, are gathered in Walter M. Abbott, S.J., ed., *The Documents of Vatican II* (New York: America Press, 1966).

Particular writers have influenced parts of this book. Edmund Campion, Catholic priest, church historian, and friend, helped me through his writing. His *A Place in the City* (Ringwood, Victoria: Penguin Books Australia, 1994) deepened my appreciation for the living presence of the saints. His *Rockchoppers: Growing Up Catholic in Australia* (Ringwood, Victoria: Penguin Books Australia, 1982) inspired the conclusion and helped me make sense of my own story. John Dunne, C.S.C., has helped me understand better the connection between suffering and the capacity to love. See in particular his *The Church of the Poor Devil: Reflections on a Riverboat Voyage and a Spiritual Journey* (New York: Macmillan, 1982), and *The Reasons of the Heart: A*

Journey Into Solitude and Back Again Into the Human Circle (Notre Dame: University of Notre Dame Press, 1979). I benefited much from the poem-prayers of Michael Leunig, one of which I quote in the reflection on "Faith Across the Generations." See his *A Common Prayer* (North Blackburn, Victoria: Collins Dove, 1990); and *The Prayer Tree* (North Blackburn, Victoria: Collins Dove, 1991). Louis Lavelle, *Four Saints: The Meaning of Holiness* (Notre Dame: University of Notre Dame Press, 1963), provides further insight into the marvelous Francis of Assisi.

I borrow from some of my own previously published work in a couple of the reflections. The essay on St. Francis relies heavily on sections of my "Contrasts in the Likeness of Christ," *Living Prayer*, Vol. 20, No. 4 (July-August 1987), pp. 20-26. The essay on the need for Catholic politicians draws upon two articles: "The Tragedy of Mario Cuomo," *Notre Dame Magazine*, Vol. 22, No. 3 (Autumn 1993), pp. 41-43; and "The Public Servant [Robert P. Casey]," *Notre Dame Magazine*, Vol. 24, No. 2 (Summer 1995), pp. 20-22.

Other books and articles which influenced my thinking on specific subjects include: Neil Howe and William Straus, *Generations: The History of America's Future, 1584-2069* (New York: Morrow, 1991); David Walley, *Teenage Nervous Breakdown: Music and Politics in the Post-Elvis Age* (New York: Insight Books, 1998); Andrew Delbanco, *The Death of Satan: How Americans Have Lost the Sense of Evil* (New York: Farrar, Straus and Giroux, 1995); Mary Patricia Barth Fourqurean, "Chastity as Shared Strength: An Open Letter to Students," *America* (November 6, 1993), pp. 10-14; Michael Garvey, "The Scary Fidelity of Jesus: What Makes Marriage Possible?" *Commonweal* (March 24, 1989), pp. 173-74; Christopher Lasch with Elizabeth Lasch-Quinn, *Women and the Common Life: Love, Marriage, and Feminism* (New York: Norton, 1997); Catherine Mowry LaCugna, "Catholic Women as Ministers and Theologians," *America*, (October 10, 1992), pp. 238-48; Patrick Arnold, "In Search of the Hero: Masculine Spirituality and Liberal Christianity,"

America (October 7, 1989), pp. 206-10; Robert Bellah, et al., *Habits of the Heart: Individualism and Commitment in American Life* (Berkeley: University of California Press, 1985); Margaret O'Brien Steinfels, 1991 Commencement Address, University of Notre Dame, *Notre Dame Report* (June 14, 1991), pp. 396-99; George McKenna, "On Abortion: A Lincolnian Position," *The Atlantic Monthly* (September 1995), pp. 51-68; Marshall Frady, "Death in Arkansas," *The New Yorker* (February 22, 1993), pp. 105-33; Richard John Neuhaus, *The Catholic Moment: The Paradox of the Church in the Postmodern World* (San Francisco: Harper & Row, 1987); Vincent Nichols, "A Vision for Every Child," *The Tablet Education Supplement* (February 13, 1999), pp. 209-11; Abigail Thernstrom, "Out-classed: Why Parochial Schools Beat Public Ones," *The New Republic* (May 13, 1991), pp. 12-14.

I drew on Robert Bolt's *A Man for All Seasons* (New York: SBS, 1960) and Kathleen Norris's *Dakota: A Spiritual Geography* (Boston: Houghton Mifflin, 1993) in specific ways in this book, but each work served as a more broad influence upon me. I commend both to readers.